WANDERLUST IN BERLIN

*An insider's guide to the best places
to eat, drink and explore*

JULIAN TOMPKIN

Hardie Grant

TRAVEL

WANDERLUST
IN BERLIN

*An insider's guide to the best places
to eat, drink and explore*

JULIAN TOMPKIN

CONTENTS

WELCOME TO WANDERLUST IN BERLIN

It was the opening years of the new millennium and I was hurtling on a train from Berlin's weary Schönefeld Airport towards the city centre: Mitte. What I remember most vividly are the cranes: thousands of cranes pirouetting as if in some finely choreographed primordial dance. It was living theatre in its truest form: you could sit with a beer in a makeshift bar on an abandoned terrace still pockmarked with bullet-holes and watch the city being resurrected, brick by brick.

But Berlin is not a city that grows on you: it grows in you. Few are instantly 'wowed' by its cosmetic character: the full cataclysm of 20th-century barbarism was unleashed here on these cobbled streets in unmerciful fashion, leaving a once impressive city ravaged, buckled and quartered post-World War II. This absence of superficiality is what makes Berlin such an extraordinary place today. It has emerged as a creative powerhouse in just a few short decades ... and its story is still being written. The paint of history is so wet here that it's impossible not to get it on your skin.

The Berlin of the 21st century is a model of tolerance – having perhaps, in the (paraphrased) words of 19th-century philosopher Friedrich Nietzsche, gazed into the abyss for so long it eventually found the abyss gazing back and is now determined to set the record straight. This has gifted Berliners with an amazing appetite for life: it's a city of bars and boutiques, galleries and gastronomy, history and hedonism. It's one of the most creative destinations on the planet – bursting at the seams with artists, galleries, museums and street art. And it's also one of the world's truly green cities, surrounded by bucolic lakes and forests and speckled with verdurous gardens and parks.

Berlin brings out the wanderlust in us all: a city in which to get lost and in which to get found.

Der Weg ist das Ziel ... the journey is the reward.

Julian

ABOUT BERLIN

Berlin's multifarious personality is what makes it wholly unique: a city ripe with contradictions, which is at once ancient yet contemporary, scruffy yet arcadian, traditional yet radical, formal yet irreverent.

Once the capital of the Prussian empire, once a ruin after its nefarious turn with Nazism, once a city divided by the Cold War, today Berlin has faced up to its past and is again a model of tolerance and refuge: a bastion of multiculturalism, progressive political thought and social justice. It's a city of a little more than 3.5 million inhabitants, reverberating in creativity, character and vitality.

History can be quite the chameleon. Browse its annals prior to the late Middle Ages and Berlin – then little more than a muddy village in Europe's northern frontier land – barely rates a drop of ink. What we now know as Berlin is in fact the inheritance of two small Slavic villages, Berlin and Cölln – both precariously clinging to a tiny archipelago in the River Spree. It now encompasses the borough of Mitte, featuring the Nikolaiviertel (see p.83), Museum Island (see p.69) and the Fischerinsel (what remains of the ancient settlement of Cölln, see p.69). The outlying Brandenburg villages of Spandau and Köpenick – now integral parts of Berlin – first appear in historical documents around the same time, all dating back to the 12th century.

The area was the fractious fiefdom of local warlords (including Slavs, Bohemians and Teutons), amongst them Jaxa of Köpenick: the final Slavic ruler before the Germanic Albert the Bear wrestled control in the 12th century, thus proclaiming it the Margraviate of Brandenburg principality. The Slavic Wends (known locally as Sorbs) gifted Berlin its name: Brlo, which loosely translates to 'habitable place in marshland' – and Jaxa's Sorbian inheritors remain in the region to this day, most notably in the Spreewald region south of Berlin, famed for its sublime gherkins and network of idyllic waterways.

Berlin remained relatively inconspicuous – a backwater, traded amongst the European gentry and Teutonic Knights – until 1410, when Roman Emperor Sigismund gifted the Margraviate to an ambitious dynasty from southern

ABOUT BERLIN

Germany, the Hohenzollerns, which ruled until the end of World War I. In 1415, Friedrich IV of Nuremberg became Friedrich I of Brandenburg, and within two centuries the region had – through intermarriage with Baltic nobles – metamorphosed into the Kingdom of Prussia: one of world history's leading players.

This pristine and wild expanse of forest and lakes suddenly found itself embroidered with resplendent palaces and manors. The bridle trail between Potsdam and Berlin was renamed Schlossstrasse (Palace Road), linking the regal nerve centres of this quickly expanding empire that would, at its zenith in the 18th and 19th centuries, reach from Belgium to Lithuania. Under 18th-century ruler Friedrich the Great, Prussia evolved into one of the world's most formidable – and feared – militarised states, earning the Prussians a reputation for being both cunning and imperialistic: contradicted by Friedrich's deep love of art, and his quest to make Berlin a global epicentre of the Enlightenment.

Throughout the centuries, Berlin had a reputation as a city of tolerance and refuge: opening its fortified city gates to the persecuted and exiled, including French Huguenots, Protestant Bohemians and Moravians and Jewish peoples expelled from Russia's Pale of Settlement.

Prussia became the mightiest power in Europe following victories against Austria and France in 1871, and Berlin soon found itself the capital of a newly unified Germany – with Wilhelm I crowned its head as German Emperor. His eventual successor Wilhelm II, however, would steer Prussia and its capital towards wreck and ruin. Germany ended World War I in total defeat, with the abdication of Wilhelm II and the end of the Hohenzollern dynasty, the dismantling of the Prussian state and the 1919 *Treaty of Versailles* reparations that would cripple the optimism of the Weimar Republic (1918–33) ... and arguably portend the rise of Nazism.

Nazi atrocities would be avenged with the near erasure of the city centre, with scant little remaining to speak of its ancient history beyond charred and skeletal ruins. Today there are few survivors: amongst them the *Totendanz (Dance of Death)* frieze in the Marienkirche (St Mary's Church, see p.83) an ancient and auspicious prophecy of this city's often all-too fatalistic flirtations with doom.

Post-World War II, the Cold War saw Berlin quartered by the Allies: dividing kin and fellow Berlin citizens behind the concrete Berlin Wall for nearly 30 years and creating a city with two distinct and often incongruous personalities. East Berlin gazed east beyond the Vistula River to Russia, and West Berlin gazed west beyond the Rhine. The 'Wende' – or peaceful revolution – in the East would triumph on 9 November 1989 when the Wall finally fell. But despite reunification in 1990, Berlin today remains a mosaic of its enigmatic history: the East and the West still evident in the most humdrum of manifestations, including the East's

ABOUT BERLIN

'Ampelmann' pedestrian light symbols – a somewhat kitsch red and green figure of a man in a hat that's transformed from a curiosity into a cultural icon – from its communist past.

Three decades on from reunification, satellite imagery still reveals the demarcation scars between the East and the West: the East warm with bronze gaslight, the West in fluorescent white. In a city with distinct kieze (neighbourhoods) and an eclectic personality, orientation is in the eye of the beholder. The River Spree cuts roughly east–west across the city and the Havel river runs north–south on the city's western fringe. The borough of Mitte (meaning middle) sits at its geographic heart, surrounded by key inner-city boroughs, including Prenzlauer Berg, Kreuzberg, Friedrichshain and Neukölln.

While populous, the city carries a relaxed air, never feels too crowded and is fabled for its clean air and abundance of lakes and green spaces. It has a fantastic public transport network of trains, trams and buses but is also notoriously flat – so it's perfect (and safe) for cycling.

Today Berlin finds itself at the epicentre of European power once more: politically and economically. Yet its affordable rents (a legacy from East German socialism, where apartments were state owned) and enduring aura of ramshackle chic have maintained its vibrancy. It's a city where history is conspicuous: where detailed information panels never shy away from the truth and brass pavement plaques called Stolpersteine (tripping stones) mark where Jewish victims of National Socialism once lived.

It's difficult to graft a Berliner: they're a people notorious for their resilience as much as their no-nonsense demeanour. Echte Berliners (real Berliners) are often characterised by their proud gruffness – what other Germans identify as the 'Berliner Schnauze' (Berliner snout): a demeanour and vernacular that is proudly unvarnished and bluntly forthright.

Gastronomy here is both avant-garde and folkish. A rich mosaic of regions, 'German cuisine' is an olio of distinct regional styles and 'Berliner Küche' (kitchen) is itself a historical pastiche, befitting its once-imperial reach and historical centre as a city of ravage, ruin and refuge.

Berlin is also a city where life is visceral. Where museums are world-renowned and art galleries cast out far beyond the cutting-edge. It has long been a magnet for artists: with around 20,000 living and working in the city today, drawn by its edginess and cheap rents. In 2005 UNESCO ordained Berlin a City of Design, and today it's home to over 700 official art galleries and a vibrant street art scene. Also boasting four world-class theatre companies, three globally renowned opera companies and the courted Philharmonic Orchestra, Berlin has been re-branded the 'The City of Art'.

Which will be your Berlin?

About

BERLIN

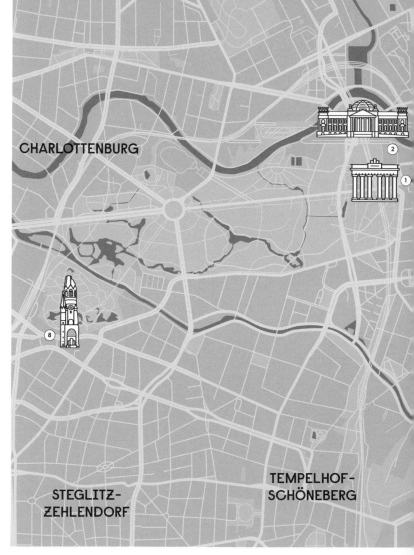

WEDDING

MITTE

MOABIT

N

CHARLOTTENBURG

Key

1. Brandenburg Gate
2. Reichstag
3. Marienkirche
4. Museum Island
5. Hackesche Höfe
6. Alexanderplatz
7. Gendarmenmarkt
8. Kaiser Wilhelm Memorial Church
9. East Side Gallery

STEGLITZ-ZEHLENDORF

TEMPELHOF-SCHÖNEBERG

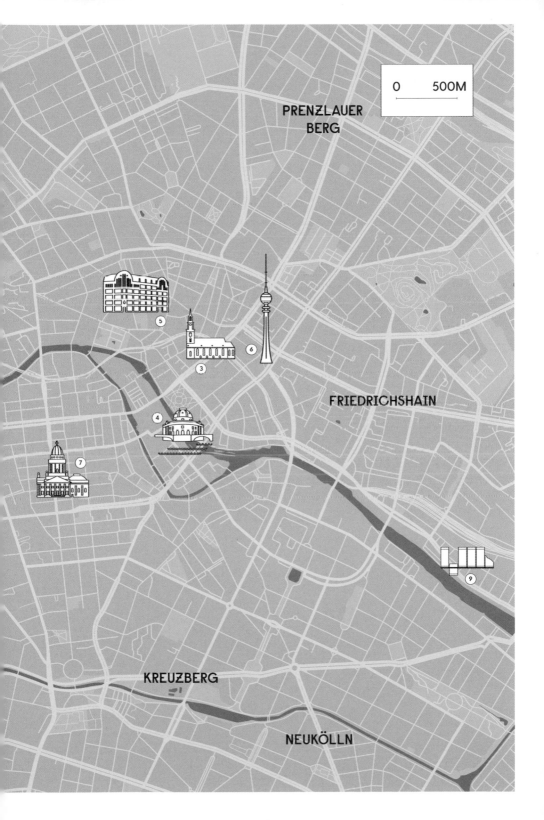

PRENZLAUER
BERG

0   500M

FRIEDRICHSHAIN

KREUZBERG

NEUKÖLLN

NEIGHBOURHOOD INDEX

NEIGHBOURHOOD INDEX

NOTABLE
NEIGHBOURHOODS

*Berlin is an unusually decentralised city – a hangover
from the days of the Berlin Wall, when it had two political
centres, two commercial hearts and two suburban sprawls.
Mitte (which literally translates as 'middle'), however, has
re-emerged as the geographical and spiritual heart of the
city and is ringed by a network of idiosyncratic suburbs
(boroughs). The entries in this book are listed by borough –
13 in total, and each with their own unique kieze (small
neighbourhoods or hubs within boroughs). Here is a brief
overview of each borough.*

MITTE
—

The historic heart of the city but also the site of its greatest destruction
following war and division, Mitte has been resurrected in the three decades
since reunification in 1990: its grand old buildings and palaces restored and
Unter den Linden (see p.85) boulevard hotwired back to life. Centred around
the ancient townships of Nikolaiviertel (see p.83), Fischerinsel (what remains
of the ancient town of Cölln) and Dorotheenstadt (around Unter den Linden),
Mitte is bundled with treasures. From the cultural Mecca that is Museum Island
(see p.69), replete with Berliner Dom (cathedral) and the rebuilt Berlin City
Palace, (see p.69) right through to the Brandenburg Gate (see p.87), Reichstag
(see p.73) and Tiergarten park (see p.201). The Gendarmenmarkt (see p.89) is
the city's most alluring square, with big-hitting Wall and war sites all a short
stroll away, including Checkpoint Charlie, the Memorial to the Murdered Jews
of Europe (see p.77) and the Topography of Terror (see p.71). To the north lies
Alexanderplatz (see p.81), as well as the bustling Hackescher Markt (see p.183)
quarter: once home to a thriving Jewish population.

Neighbourhoods

NOTABLE NEIGHBOURHOODS

KREUZBERG
—

Once the frontier of West Berlin, today Kreuzberg is perhaps the city's most iconic borough and wears its swagger with ease: a heady mix of urbane Berliners, a thriving Turkish community and a large cohort of other expats. With its borders defined by the River Spree to the north – beyond which was East Berlin – Kreuzberg has always been a centre of progressive art, radical politics and anti-Establishment ferment. Post reunification, some of its more fetching quarters were quick to gentrify – including the charming Bergmannkiez (see p.189) and Graefekiez: both bundled with sophisticated eateries, boutiques and bars. But despite its upscale spit and polish, Kreuzberg's heart still beats to a countercultural drumbeat. Kottbusser Tor boasts some of the city's finest Turkish restaurants, including Doyum Restaurant (see p.117). The resurrected Markthalle Neun markets (see p.167), to the east of the borough, has become its culinary epicentre: bursting with international street food and craft beer. The Paul-Lincke-Ufer laneway along the Landwehr Canal is one of the city's best places for a stroll or bankside picnic on a warm day.

PRENZLAUER BERG
—

Prenzlauer Berg's Wilhelmine-era buildings miraculously survived the Allied bombs of World War II and today the borough is laden with international eateries, boutiques and markets. East Berlin dissidents would eventually engineer the Wende (peaceful revolution) from Prenzlauer Berg – so when the Wall fell, it fell here: at the Bösebrucke (Bornholmer Bridge) crossing. Artists and revolutionaries quickly flooded the tenements – transforming the area, for a time, into a countercultural squatter's republic (even removing street signs to disorient West German police unfamiliar with the area). But before long the developers moved in and the suburb's iconic Wilhelmine grandeur was restored. The Kollwitzkiez, Helmholtzkiez, Kastanienallee (see p.191) quarter and the Winsviertel are all stunning neighbourhoods to explore. Must-see sites include Mauerpark Flea Market (see p.171), Gethsemanekirche (from where the Wende began), Rykestrasse Synagogue and Jewish Cemetery, as well as the Bösebrucke and Kollwitzplatz Farmers' Markets (see p.169), which take place each Saturday.

NOTABLE NEIGHBOURHOODS

NEUKÖLLN
—

Neukölln's transformation to hipster-central caught many off-guard. Once an inconspicuous area of Germanic working class and a large Turkish community, today the area has metamorphosed. With Kreuzberg's rents surging, Berlin's international youth-set and student hordes began spilling over into Neukölln. The area has quickly gained a reputation for its bolthole natural wine bars such as Jaja (see p.157), trend-conscious denizens, unconventional boutiques and its cutting-edge international food scene led by the likes of Palsta (see p.129). Neukölln began life as the village of Rixdorf and had an 18th-century reputation for gambling, boozing and prostitution. It later changed its name to Neukölln – after the medieval town of Cölln. The area boasts the historic Richardplatz: the preserved village centre of old Rixdorf, dating back to the 17th century.

FRIEDRICHSHAIN
—

Friedrichshain and Kreuzberg may be one administrative borough, but these two neighbouring suburbs – divided by the River Spree (and once divided by a concrete wall) – couldn't be more at odds. Taking its name from Prussian history's favoured ruler, Friedrich the Great, the borough was bludgeoned by World War II (when briefly its name was changed to Horst-Wessel-Stadt after the 'martyred' Nazi stormtrooper). The Soviets centred on Friedrichshain for much of their public works, including the socialist neoclassical architecture of Stalinallee, now Karl-Marx-Allee. While parts of Friedrichshain maintain a socialist feel, the area around Boxhagener Platz (see p.195) has emerged as one of the city's liveliest kieze (neighbourhoods), with edgy bars, eateries and boutiques: and a fabled flea market (see p.177). The RAW Tempel – a ruined rail work-yard and bomb shelter – is today a centre of graffiti art. And the East Side Gallery (see p.95) remains one of the city's most visited and moving Berlin Wall sites.

Neighbourhoods

CHARLOTTENBURG
—

So enamoured was Kaiser Friedrich I with his second wife Sophia Charlotte he renamed her favourite palace – the Lietzenburg (see p.209) – in her honour on her death in 1705. The area would later emerge as inner-Berlin's most affluent borough with stunning 19th-century apartments and West Berlin's most luxurious shopping street, the Kurfürstendamm (see p.197). The Kaufhaus des Westens (Department store of the West, see p.59) – better known as KaDeWe – became the very emblem of opulence in the early 20th century. The advent of the Berlin Wall saw Charlottenburg also emerge as a centre for art and culture; still home today to the Deutsche Oper Berlin, Theater des Westens, Helmut Newton Foundation and Käthe Kollwitz Museum. Following reunification Charlottenburg fell into quietude, but today is once again back under stage light thanks to Bikini Berlin (see p.197): the city's trendiest shopping address. Despite its modish turn, Charlottenburg maintains its air of fin de siècle grace, with headline attractions including the war-damaged Kaiser Wilhelm Memorial Church (see p.97) and Berlin's world-famous zoo in the Tiergarten (see p.201).

WEDDING
—

Oh, how a decade can change everything: for Wedding has finally emerged in recent years from shabby borough to one of Berlin's hippest addresses. While its evolution is far from complete, Wedding promises one of the city's best bar scenes – with a number of unconventional eateries such as MARS (see p.62) and tucked-away galleries. The borough wears an air of worn grace: its grand old apartments (including examples of post-war modernism) are largely untouched by the hand of gentrification. One such apartment was once home to the married couple Otto and Elsie Hampel, whose quiet and heroic resistance against the Nazi machine (the distribution of postcards criticising Hitler) lead to their brutal execution: their story inspiring one of Berlin's landmark works of literature, *Alone in Berlin* (also known as *Every Man Dies Alone*) by Hans Fallada (see p.221) – published in 1947. The diminutive Panke River is a true icon of the borough, with its verdant stretches of walking paths.

TEMPELHOF-SCHÖNEBERG
—

Tempelhof-Schöneberg has been home to a rollcall of famous names: David Bowie and Iggy Pop lived here in their most seminal days; it is the birthplace of arch-Berlin icons Marlene Dietrich and Helmut Newton; and was the long-time home to Albert Einstein. But Schöneberg dates back to the 13th century and has long exuded an air of sophistication. It's also long been a fierce battle-ground of progressive social ideals: predominately as the epicentre of Berlin's LGBTIQ+ community. Indeed, one of the city's most famous gay residents – Christopher Isherwood – penned *The Berlin Stories* here (see p.221): what would later be adapted into *Cabaret*. The imposing Rathaus Town Hall was the site of John F. Kennedy's historic *'Ich bin ein Berliner'* speech ('I am a citizen of Berlin'). Today Schöneberg offers contemporary eateries such as Mana (see p.65), sophisticated bars and many local boutiques. It's an administrative union with Tempelhof: best known for its historic airport (and site of the Cold War-era Berlin Airlift), now a truly unique public park known as Tempelhofer Feld (see p.211).

MOABIT
—

Whilst today it maintains a distinctly Alt Berlin (Old Berlin) feel – unbothered by fad and fashion – Moabit was once the centre of the city's breakneck industrialisation of the early 19th century. The area soon developed into a working-class borough, most distinguished for its eponymous prison. The construction of the Berlin Wall saw Moabit demoted to a low-profile fringe borough of West Berlin: a sentiment that would outlast the Wall, well into the 21st century. Today it's replete with kneipe (working class pubs with unfussy food, quickly disappearing in other boroughs) and still proudly boasts one of the city's last 19th-century market halls, the Arminiusmarkthalle (Markthalle X) (see p.179). Bound 360 degrees by water and lined with handsome apartment blocks of yesteryear, however, this borough is a secret no longer, with signs of gentrification increasingly evident. Moabit was also the site of Kommune I: Berlin's most notorious 1960s commune and a haven of free sex, drug experimentation and a radical political agenda.

NOTABLE NEIGHBOURHOODS

STEGLITZ-ZEHLENDORF

–

This sprawling borough in the south of Berlin encompasses most of the city's well-heeled addresses: amongst them Lichterfelde, Zehlendorf, Dahlem and Wannsee. Here cobbled laneways lined with every shade of Porsche, Audi, BMW and Mercedes are festooned with luxurious 19th- and early 20th-century mansions and surrounded by pristine lakes and plush forest. Whilst Steglitz is the area's commercial heart, the southern lake district is where most Berliners come to play: namely the Wannsee lake (see p.213), with its historic open-air lido, or Strandbad, and imported beach sand. At the heart of this borough is the enigmatic Grunewald forest, with its network of lakes: most famous being the Schlachtensee (see p.215) with its much-loved Fischerhütte restaurant and beer garden (see p.137). The borough is also home to countless heavy-hitting sites: the Expressionist Brücke Museum (see p.99); Impressionist painter Max Liebermann's stately home, now a gallery and cafe (see p.213); and the House of the Wannsee Conference, where Nazis convened in January 1942 to formalise 'the Final Solution'.

TREPTOW-KÖPENICK

–

Berlin's most south-eastern corner, Treptow-Köpenick is an idyll of lakes, waterways and historic sites. It's here that the River Spree washes into Berlin's largest lake, the Müggelsee, and converges with the Dahme river, in one of the city's most enchanting settings. At its most inner reach, the borough is defined by Treptower Park (see p.217): one of Berlin's most iconic open spaces, fringing the River Spree and home to the grandiose Soviet War Memorial. In recent years Treptow and nearby Baumschulenweg have seen an influx of creatives from adjoining Kreuzberg: attracted by affordable warehouse spaces and green surrounds, where many Berliners keep Schrebergärten (garden allotments). To the east, at the confluence of the two rivers, sits Köpenick (see p.101): one of Berlin's ancient settlements – with its village-like allure, striking town hall and eponymous palace. At the city's most eastern point is Rahnsdorf: an ancient fishing village served by a historic and truly idiosyncratic tramway (Woltersdorf Tramway) that cuts through the pristine Köpenick Forest.

NOTABLE NEIGHBOURHOODS

SPANDAU

–

Spandau's old town is enigmatically perched on a small island at the confluence of the rivers Spree and Havel. One of Berlin's original medieval villages, Spandau has maintained its historic allure despite war and segregation. The Altstadt (old town) is a network of cobbled lanes lined with old-time cafes and eateries: many with prime water frontage. At its centre stands the Saint Nicholas Church, where in 1539 Kurfürst Joachim II Hector first took Protestant communion, thus rerouting the future of Prussia and Germany. The borough's landmark site, however, is its eponymous citadel, Zitadelle Spandau (see p.103) – an awe-inspiring masterwork of renaissance architecture that is today both a museum and a spectacular setting for outdoor concerts. Spandau was also famed for its historic prison, whose most notorious prisoners were the Nazi chieftains Albert Speer and Rudolf Hess, the latter who committed suicide in the prison in 1987, aged 93. The building was demolished soon afterwards to prevent it becoming a Nazi shrine.

POTSDAM

–

While not officially part of Berlin (Berlin is a city state and Potsdam is the capital of the separate federal state of Brandenburg), Potsdam is just a few kilometres outside Berlin's city boundaries and innately tethered to Berlin's history – and is where the Hohenzollern dynasty built some of its finest regal palaces, which you can still enjoy today. It is connected to the city's suburban rail networks and makes for a rewarding day trip. Friedrich the Great built his favourite palace here, Sanssouci Palace (see p.105), which was completed in 1747, and several more palaces followed – including the Neues Palais, Charlottenhof and Orangerieschloss – and a charming town emerged at the centre. Today the city is home to historic Dutch and Russian quarters and is also the site of the Cecilienhof Palace, where Winston Churchill, Harry S. Truman and Joseph Stalin convened in 1945 to carve up Germany, in what became known as the Potsdam Conference. Potsdam is also home to Babelsberg Studio and Filmpark: an icon of cinema and where Fritz Lang crafted the iconic *Metropolis* (1927).

SUMMER:
OLD BERLIN
FULL-DAY ITINERARY

Berlin may have a reputation as a vibrant 21st-century city, but its known
origins date back to the early 12th century. This walk takes you through
the original settlements of Berlin and Cölln, revealing many concealed
landmarks and some of the city's most defining sites.

8 AM Begin the day with a revitalising breakfast of sweet potato pancakes
with chia seeds, apple and sour cherry soy dressing at ⓵ **Hackescher**
Hof Restaurant (see p.38), before admiring the resplendent Jugendstil (Art
Nouveau) courtyards (see p.75) directly outside, rendered with ornate ceramic
tiles and designed by architect August Endell in 1906.

9 AM: Stroll down An der Spandauer Brücke and onto Rosenstrasse until
you reach Karl-Liebknecht-Strasse, and cross over to the early 13th-century
⓶ **Marienkirche** (St Mary's Church, see p.83), the city's oldest surviving
church – its vestibule adorned with the faded and enigmatic *Totentanz*
(Dance of Death) mural. After exploring the church walk down Spandauer
Strasse past the 19th-century ⓷ **Neptune Fountain** towards the striking
red brick ⓸ **Town Hall**, then cross Spandauer Strasse and enter the historic
⓹ **Nikolaiviertel** (Nikolai Quarter, see p.83): the site of Berlin's original
settlement. Here you'll find the ⓺ **Nikolaikirche** – a church predating
the Marienkirche to around 1220, but which required total reconstruction,
according to its original plans, after World War II. Explore the cobbled lanes
surrounding the church and admire the architectural re-creations of Alt
Berlin (Old Berlin), before visiting the small but charming ⓻ **Ephraim-**
Palais Museum (€7/5) to explore 800 years of Berlin history in a recreated
renaissance mansion.

11 AM: Follow Propststrasse and take the riverside Spreeufer (promenade)
and cross the ⓼ **Rathausbrücke** (bridge) onto what is now known as
Fischerinsel (Fisher's Island), but was once the ancient settlement of Cölln,
opposite Berlin. Both the resurrected ⓽ **Berlin City Palace** (see p.69) and
baroque ⑩ **Neuer Marstall** (royal stables, now an elite music academy)
can be admired from here. Turn left onto Breite Strasse and pass in front
of the distinctive ⑪ **Ribbeck-Haus**: Berlin's only original renaissance-era
house, dating from 1624. Turn right onto Neumannsgasse and then left onto
Brüderstrasse where you'll find two historic houses: the ⑫ **Galgenhaus**,
built in 1688 and the ⑬ **Nicolaihaus**, built in 1674. Then take the historic
⑭ **Jungfernbrücke** footbridge, which is Berlin's oldest bridge, dating from

the 1680s, and turn right and follow the path along the river to Unter den Linden, and turn left. Note the restored Staatsoper (see 8pm) on your left and turn right onto Universitätstrasse to the imposing ⑮ **Humboldt University** building, where Albert Einstein taught – taking note of the monument of Friedrich the Great astride a horse in the middle of the road.

12.30PM Continue along Universitätstrasse to the corner of Georgenstrasse, where you'll find the old munitions storeroom ⑯ **Deponie Nr. 3** (see p.142), now a unique cavernous brasserie beneath the rail line where you can enjoy a revitalising beer and the choice of many Berlin specialty dishes, including classics such as Kohlroulade: rolled cabbage with pork and gravy.

2PM Walk back along Universitätstrasse to Unter den Linden. To the left you will find the ⑰ **Deutsches Historisches Museum** (German History Museum, €8/4) fronting onto the River Spree, with its engaging exhibitions tracing the rollicking history of this nation and its once independent duchies and kingdoms.

4PM East along Unter den Linden you'll find various highlights of the street, such as the ⑱ **Neue Wache** memorial (featuring Käthe Kollwitz' moving sculpture *Mother with Dead Son*, see p.85) and the Nazi book burning site at ⑲ **Bebelplatz** (see p.85). Walk west along the street around 1km (0.6mi) to arrive at Pariser Platz and the historic ⑳ **Brandenburg Gate** (see p.87): the city's most iconic city gate, and a major Cold War flashpoint. Turn right on Ebertstrasse then left onto Scheidemannstrasse where you'll find the entrance to the ㉑ **Reichstag** (see p.73): Germany's national parliament (tickets are free but due to its popularity and tight security they need to be pre-booked online in advance). Explore the building's iconic domed roof with a photo exhibition detailing its storied past.

6.30PM Return to Unter den Linden via Ebertstrasse and head to the ㉒ **Hotel Adlon** (see p.113) to enjoy a uniquely Berlin meal with a luxurious twist, such as a döner kebab with truffle cream, in the Lobby Bar of Berlin's most elegant hotel, replete with marble sculptures and shimmering chandeliers.

8PM If you have energy reserves, catch a rousing Germanic opera from Beethoven, Mozart, Wagner or Strauss at one of Berlin's world-renowned opera houses, of which there are two on Unter den Linden: the ㉓ **Staatsoper** (classic repertoire) and ㉔ **Komische Oper** (opera, operetta and musicals). End the night with a glass of unforgettable German wine and late-night nibbles at ㉕ **Cordo** (see p.112). After a full day of walking, you may want to take a taxi to get there.

SCHEIDEMANNSTRASSE

DOROTHEEN STRASSE

EBERTSTRASSE

AUTUMN:
WAR AND WALL
FULL-DAY ITINERARY

*War consumed Berlin throughout the 20th century – both world wars and
the Cold War. What was a city left in chaos after two devastating world wars
soon became two cities divided into East and West – with the Berlin Wall
lasting from 1961–1989, with reunification finally being realised in 1990.
This walk takes in key historic sites of that catastrophic century of war and
post-World War II division.*

8AM Kick off the day with some Smørrebrød (rye bread laden with smoked
salmon, mackerel and gherkin) at ① **1687 restaurant**, with its elegant fin
de siècle grace, cosy green Chesterfields and historic artworks.

9AM Head to the city's most famed street, Unter den Linden (see p.85),
and turn left to pass in front of the historic ② **Hotel Adlon** (the city's most
iconic hotel where many a personality has frequented: from Charlie Chaplin
to Marlene Dietrich, see p.113) and continue down Wilhelmstrasse. Turn right
onto Behrenstrasse, where you'll soon reach the sobering ③ **Memorial to
the Murdered Jews of Europe** (see p.77): a forest of tomb-like concrete
structures with oscillating perspectives that will leave you feeling both moved
and unsettled.

10.30AM Double back on Behrenstrasse then stroll south on Wilhelmstrasse
past ④ **Detlev-Rohwedder-Haus** (the former office of the Nazi air force
command under Hermann Göring, embellished during the Cold War with a
utopic Soviet mural in its undercroft) to the ⑤ **Topography of Terror** (see
p.71) – a moving and confronting exploration of the crimes of the Nazi era on
the site of the now erased SS command, beside one of the final remnants of
the Berlin Wall.

12PM Turn left on Zimmerstrasse past the colourful ⑥ **Trabant Museum**
(an irreverent celebration of East Germany's iconic automobile) to
⑦ **Checkpoint Charlie**: a flashpoint of Cold War tension, with a number
of information panels and kitsch photo opportunities with costumed soldiers.

1PM Turn left onto Friedrichstrasse and right onto Jägerstrasse, then
stroll towards the Gendarmenmarkt square and the ⑧ **Augustiner am
Gendarmenmarkt beerhall**, which is the perfect pitstop for a hard-earned
tipple and plate of nourishing crispy pork knuckle lavished with German
senf (mustard). If you're lucky you'll witness (and sample) the ceremonial

tapping of a new wooden barrel of their famous Edelstoff lager, followed by rapturous applause.

2.30PM Pass through handsome and historic ⑨ **Gendarmenmarkt** square (see p.89), with its French and German churches – and head north on Markgrafenstrasse to Behrenstrasse and turn right. On your left you will come to ⑩ **Bebelplatz** (see p.85): the site of the most notorious Nazi book burning ceremony in 1933, with a subterranean memorial of empty bookshelves visible through a window underfoot. Cross Unter den Linden and enjoy a quiet moment of reflection at the ⑪ **Neue Wache** (see p.85), an early 19th-century Prussian guard tower designed by Karl Friedrich Schinkel – now housing Käthe Kollwitz's moving anti-war memorial. Walk west on the Unter den Linden to Friedrichstrasse and turn right. Continue on to the ⑫ **Friedrichstrasse Rail Station** – once known as the 'Palace of Tears', as it was the official entry point for West Berliners visiting (and eventually farewelling) family and friends in the East. A moving memorial sits outside the station to the Jewish children of Europe deported during World War II.

4PM Enter the Friedrichstrasse rail station (S-Bahn) and take either line S1 or S2 north for two stations to Nordbahnhof. Alight here and visit the fascinating ⑬ **Berlin Wall Memorial and Documentation Centre** (see p.93) on Bernauer Strasse, which begins right outside the station and slowly works its way up Bernauer Strasse with a series of information panels and interactive audio points. The Documentation Centre is directly across the road from the Wall near Nordbahnhof.

6PM Once the Memorial concludes, continue along Bernauer Strasse, turn right onto Oderberger Strasse and left onto Kastanienallee: where you can enjoy a welcome drink in the historic ⑭ **Prater Garten** (see p.153), a site of much frivolity and political ferment over the centuries.

7.30PM Backtrack a few metres down Kastanienallee, turn left onto Oderberger Strasse and right onto Schönhauser Allee and stroll on to ⑮ **Fleischerei** – a former butcher-cum-German restaurant in the heartland of old East Berlin, where Brandenburg beef is king and many German classics – such as the schnitzel – are given a sophisticated contemporary makeover.

WINTER:
CITY OF STREET ART
HALF-DAY ITINERARY

Berlin has defined itself as a city of art and it never disappoints. While packed with galleries (both public and private), it is also a haven for international street art. Winter is a thrilling time to explore these colourful murals, which contrast so vividly against the monochrome sky.

8AM Start the day at one of the city's finest coffee roasters and breakfast haunts, ① **Zazza Kaffeehaus** (see p.39) – in one of Berlin's hippest hoods, Kreuzberg: replete with ample graffiti.

9AM Walk north on Kottbusser Damm, cross the River Spree and then take Mariannenstrasse on the right – where, soon after the intersection with Skalitzer Strasse, you'll find ② *The Astronaut* on the left: a mega painting engulfing an entire apartment-side by French artist Victor Ash. Take a right onto Oranienstrasse and you'll pass Belgian artist ③ **ROA's confronting mural** of animals strung up to the wall on the left-hand side, at the corner of Oranienstrasse and Skalitzer Strasse. Continue east down Skalitzer Strasse to Schlesisches Tor U-Bahn Rail Station and turn right onto Oppelner Strasse, where on the right-hand side you'll soon happen upon a striking ④ **mural** of a yellow-faced androgynous character by Brazilian street art twins Os Gemeos. Double back on Oppelner Strasse to Oberbaumstrasse and, as you reach the river, you'll find one of the city's more striking works of street art on the right-hand side: ⑤ *Backjump* by Italian graffiti artist Blu.

11AM Cross the River Spree on the Oberbaumbrücke bridge (where you may well find street artists spruiking original works), then turn left onto Mühlenstrasse and the beginning of the ⑥ **East Side Gallery** (see p.95): the world's largest street-art gallery etched upon one of the remaining remnants of the Berlin Wall.

1PM Double back down Mühlenstrasse and turn left onto Warschauer Strasse. When you've crossed the rail lines stroll a little further, then take the stairs behind the currywurst stand on your right down to the ⑦ **RAW Tempel**: where you can warm up at the ⑧ **Urban Spree indoor art gallery** over a glühwein (mulled wine) before moving on to pursue the eclectic, striking and most-often anonymous street art festooning the walls across the expanse of this bombed-out rail yard.

SPRING:
GREEN BERLIN

HALF-DAY ITINERARY

Berlin may have a reputation for its ruins and ramshackle chic but the city is also one of the greenest in Europe – encircled by bucolic lakes and forests. But you don't need to head to the fringes to find nature, as the city's urban centre is also defined by water and parks.

9AM Kick off the day with an inspired breakfast at ① **Café Mugrabi** (see p.41). The hummus sabich is the go-to: with creamy hummus, grilled eggplant and potatoes, and a medley of North African spices and salsas.

10AM Walk left down Görlitzer Strasse and enter ② **Görlitzer Park** at the corner of Oppelner Strasse. Walk to the middle of the park and take the walking trail left until you reach the ③ **Landwehr Canal**, taking note of the inner-city animal farm on the right – complete with horses, sheep and boisterous roosters. The Landwehr Canal was built in the mid-19th century as a shipping route, but today is one of the city's most picturesque waterways: and a favourite space for offhand graffiti work on its stone banks.

10.30AM Descend the stairs and follow Görlitzer Ufer (which becomes Heckmannufer) to ④ **Puschkinallee**, with its famous arches of trees. Cross the street and then turn right, taking note of the charming waterside wooden shacks as you cross two canals: popular swimming zones in the early 20th century – and today home to the ⑤ **Badeschiff** outdoor swimming pool and 'beach bar': a chic spot to bathe and booze, with a much-coveted cocktail bar.

11AM Continue down Puschkinallee until you reach Treptower Park S-Bahn rail station, then veer left to enter ⑥ **Treptower Park** (see p.217), until you reach the River Spree. Follow the plane tree-lined path along the River Spree and enjoy the enchanting scenery until you come to the bridge connecting to the ⑦ **Insel der Jugend** (Island of the Youth), where you can hire a row boat. Alternatively, explore the park on foot, including the colossal ⑧ **Soviet War Memorial**.

1PM Return back through Treptower Park and down Puschkinallee and cross over the first canal – the ⑨ **Flutgraben**, which is famed for the artist studios that line its waters. Turn right, taking the trail beside the petrol station where you'll find the historic ⑩ **Freischwimmer bar and eatery** (see p.161), where you can easily while away the afternoon over a German beer or wine in one of the city's most unique waterside settings, whilst contemplating a plate-sized Weiner schnitzel with potato and cucumber salad.

Treptower Park

MORGENS

– morning –

Good morning! Berlin is a habitually late-riser and the early hours can have a compelling quietude about them – until the street sweepers move in and rouse the city into life. Many cafes and shops unbolt their doors as late as 10am: when the brunch takers and all-night ravers convene over the prototypal Berliner brunch of antipasti, cheese, bread and a heart-starting cup of caffeine. Berlin's 'third wave' of coffee culture ignited a highly caffeinated revolt across the city once notorious for its no-frills percolated brews and supersized goblets of milchkaffee (coffee with milk): now demanding not only perfect barista-brewed coffee but premium, ethical ingredients whose provenance can be clearly traced. Bonanza Coffee Roasters (see p. 43) leads the way. It wasn't that long ago you couldn't find a poached egg to save your life (quite literally for those stumbling famished out of one of the city's notorious all-night dance clubs), but today the city is flush for choice. You'll be hard pressed to decide between shakshuka at Café Mugrabi (see p. 41) and huevos rancheros at Geist Im Glas (see p. 53).

House Of Small Wonder

A buttered slice of Brooklyn right in the heart of old Berlin.

When House of Small Wonder first fired up the burners in New York, specifically Williamsburg, Brooklyn, in 2010, they knew they were onto something – with the folksy wood-heavy setting decorated with planters and a menu bringing together Japanese, American and Euro influences: and starring an all-day brunch and cocktail list. So when founders Motoko Watanabe and Shaul Margulies decided to fashion a second site, über-hip Berlin was the obvious choice: with the House Of Small Wonder, known as HOSM, setting up shop just off the hubbub of Friedrichstrasse in 2014.

Once landmarked by debris, cranes and the legendary Tacheles artist squat and studio – formerly housed in the ruins of a bombed-out department store – the area surrounding Oranienburger Strasse and Torstrasse has emerged as somewhat of a foodie haven in recent years, with House of Small Wonder bringing some welcome Brooklyn flair.

With its doll-house-like winding wooden staircase and comfortable aesthetic, this haunt has given Berlin a whole new perspective on breakfast. Now every day deserves to kick off with a soboro don (ground chicken with sweet Japanese scrambled egg, rice, spinach and pickled ginger) and toasted with an umeshu-infused gin and tonic!

📍 Johannisstrasse 20

🕓 Mon–Sun
9am–11pm

€ €8–22

📞 27 58 28 77

W houseofsmallwonder.de

🚌 U-Bahn Oranienburger Tor,
S-Bahn Oranienburger Strasse

Hackescher Hof Restaurant

*Enjoy breakfast in a
historic Art Deco-inspired
wine salon.*

📍
Rosenthaler Strasse 40–1

📞
283 52 93

🚋
S-Bahn Hackescher Markt

🕐
Mon–Fri 8am–12am
Sat–Sun 9am–12am

€
€5–15

W
hackescher-hof.de

The Hackescher Hof Restaurant commands one of the most enigmatic spaces in the city. That it survived the war is a miracle in itself – made all the more profound in that it was, and remains, one of Berlin's best examples of Jugendstil (Art Nouveau) architecture and embellished by architect August Endell's fantastical tiles and decadent flourishes. It comprises a grandiose hall with preserved coffered ceilings and beguiling Art Deco finishings, such as period parquet flooring and decorative cornicing. You'll feel as though you have stepped into a bygone era, seated on burgundy leather banquettes or on wooden chairs at elegant tables covered in white cloths.

The breakfast offerings are equally alluring – try the sweet potato pancakes with chia seeds, apple and sour cherry soy dressing, and if you're a cheese lover, you can't bypass this breakfast: Fourme d'Ambert, Taleggio, Emmental, herb-infused cottage cheese, Chèvre and grape chutney.

Zazza Kaffeehaus

One of Berlin's finest coffee roasters served up in Grandma's lounge room.

📍
Schönleinstrasse 7B

📞
28 44 35 55

🚆
U-Bahn Schönleinstrasse

🕓
Mon–Sun
8.30am–8pm

€
€6–12

W
zazza-kaffee.de

Gemütlich means, at the one time, nostalgic and soul-enriching. It is a word Berliners often use to describe places unscathed by the city's frenetic 21st-century development: places without pretence. Zazza Kaffeehaus - on the quaint Hohenstaufenplatz, known for its small weekend farmers' market – is one such place. It makes you want to order a second coffee and sink into its mismatched 1950s chairs, as you admire the cake cabinets stacked sky-high, the graffiti on the exterior and traces of dust on the antiquated (but oh-so-retro) chandeliers.

While Berlin's coffee culture has been transformed beyond recognition over the last decade, it has come at an aesthetic cost: with weathered old Baltic pine floorboards and roughshod brickwork making way for taintless concrete and stainless steel. Zazza firmly plants one foot in each epoch: the best in contemporary coffee culture in a truly gemütlich Alt Berlin (Old Berlin) setting, with a headline breakfast/brunch menu, too.

Café Mugrabi

*An Israeli and North African mash-up in one
of Berlin's most diverse neighbourhoods.*

Görlitzer Park – or 'the Görli', as it's colloquially known – is at the heart of Kreuzberg's south-western fringes: a multicultural area with a melange of peoples from the four corners of the globe, which has afforded the area a distinct vibrancy and vitality. The park itself has long been a ganglion of diversity and subculture – often with a subversive edge. But while gentrification slowly chips away at the old, the area fiercely maintains its sense of multiformity: with Café Mugrabi sitting centre stage.

As hummus today has become a totem of unity, so too has shakshuka become an olive branch that transcends cast and creed. Internally the cafe is cosy and inviting with pristine white subway tiles complemented by warm wooden accents throughout – with generous light spilling in from the park beyond: perfect in winter to indulge in the traditional board games on offer. In good weather, diners spill onto the pavement tables to enjoy Café Mugrabi's legendary breakfast dishes and freshly blended juices. The hummus sabich is a perennial favourite: where creamy hummus is further anointed with grilled eggplant and potatoes and inspirited with a medley of North African spices and salsas.

Görlitzer Strasse 58

Mon–Sun 10am–5pm

€7–18

26 58 54 00

cafemugrabi.business.site

U-Bahn Schlesisches Tor

Bonanza Coffee Roasters

From bolthole to brew lab:
Berlin's coffee revolution started here.

In 2006 the 'world' came to Berlin – well, at least a significant proportion of it as the soccer World Cup descended on the city that was once the epitomic symbol of division and disunity. It was a watershed moment, kicking off an era of new-found confidence that literally infected everything: from politics to gastronomy. Emblematic of this new-found moxie was Bonanza: a hole-in-the-wall coffee joint on the fringes of Mauerpark (see p.171) that dared to dream of a Berlin beyond the ruins, late-night bars and techno clubs. Dared to dream of a sophisticated global city and a new capital of Europe.

While the legend of Bonanza's Prenzlauer Berg bolthole (known as Bonanza Coffee Heroes) lives on, the centre of its operations has now moved to Kreuzberg – home to its roastery and the purist manifestation of its bold ambition: a chic, if somewhat austere, shrine to the bean. Tucked away in a rustic courtyard set behind an urban animal farm, coffee is taken seriously here: very, very seriously (as is the tailor-ordered organic Brandenburg milk). Pensive baristas man the machines ready to dazzle and froth, and the latest in coffee paraphernalia is on show: from lavish bean-dosers and anodized aluminium barista scales (both Bluetooth-controlled, of course), to on-trend Bonanza hoodies – all to the comforting cries of the nearby cockerel. While coffee is the absolute focus here, they also spruik simple fare, such as croissants and cookies.

Adalbertstrasse 70

208 48 80 20

U-Bahn Kottbusser Tor

Mon–Fri 9am–6pm
Sat–Sun 10am–6pm

€5–10

W
bonanzacoffee.de

Anna Blume

*Berlin's brunch pioneers – where flowers and food
come together in heavenly matrimony.*

A legend has to start somewhere. While Berlin's brunch culture is
synonymous with the hard-partying-late-rising city today, two decades
ago the word 'brunch' was as foreign as kimchi and kombucha. All that
changed, however, when a florist-cum-café in Prenzlauer Berg's then slowly
rejuvenating Kollwitz kiez (neighbourhood) started offering its increasingly
urbane population what has now become Berlin culinary lore: generous layers
of regional cold cuts, cheeses, dips, fruit, condiments and wholesome seeded
breads known as an etagere (tiered plate), best shared in convivial company ...
usually accompanied by a reviving coffee.

    While Kollwitz kiez has now fully emerged as one of the city's most
affluent corners, the legend of Anna Blume lives on: and customers come
from far and wide to experience the fabled brunch etagere, available for two
or four people, and with vegetarian and now vegan options. Fringing the
equally feted Kollwitzplatz Farmer's Markets, (see p.169) long queues usually
form on the weekend – whether sunshine or snow – as people patiently wait
out a terrace table amidst the vibrant bouquets of flowers: so get in early or
visit during the week, when the street is more tranquil but no less beguiling.
Anna Blume takes its name from the oft-cited 1919 poem *An Anna Blume*, by
the surrealist inter-war artist Kurt Schwitters.

📍
Kollwitzstrasse 83

🕐
Mon–Sun 8am–10pm

€
€10–20

📞
44 04 87 49

W
cafe-anna-blume.de

🚋
Tram Prenzlauer Allee/
Danziger Strasse

Kaffee Käthe

Elegant brunch haven on one of the city's
most charming streets.

Kaffee Käthe is a welcoming place to consider the artist Käthe Kollwitz's
life and memory on one of Berlin's most alluring streetscapes – and in one
of its most coveted brunch destinations. Few figures epitomise Germany's
tumultuous 19th- and 20th-century history quite like her.

The cafe is in the borough Kollwitz once called home, and just across
from the eponymously named square, where a statue of her by Gustav
Seitz takes centre place. Enjoy resplendent brunch platters, an array of egg
dishes or a sublime selection of cake and coffee. The Käthe platter boasts a
classic selection of cheeses, ham, eggs and bread rolls paired with bircher
muesli, yoghurt, fruits and honey: the archetypal Berliner breakfast – enjoyed
either on the bustling cobbled terrace or in the elegantly minimalist interior,
beneath soft filament lighting.

Born in 1867 in East Prussia's capital Königsberg (erased from world
maps by World War II), Kollwitz was from a family with radical socialist
leanings with an antipathy to the Hohenzollern dynastic rule of Prussia and
later Nazism. The Nazis deemed her work 'Entartete Kunst' (degenerate art).
Her etchings, drawings and sculptures have documented German history:
from the German Peasants' War of 1525 to the ill-fated 1844 revolt of
Silesian weavers. Kollwitz' most enduring work is *Pietá* (known as *Mother
with Dead Son*): a deeply moving sculpture of a grieving mother holding her
lifeless son, housed today in the Neue Wache (see p.85) and inspired by the
bereavement for her own son Peter, killed in World War I.

Kollwitzstrasse 38

Mon–Fri 8am–6pm
Sat–Sun 9am–6pm

€8–15

157 73 76 40 07

kaffeekaethe.com

U-Bahn Senefelderplatz

No Fire No Glory

Nietzsche re-brewed: 'I drink coffee, therefore I am.'

While many bolthole coffee haunts have come, gone or metamorphosed since the heady days of Berlin's 'third wave' of coffee culture, No Fire No Glory has withstood the rising rents and shifting landscape – gaining a city wide following from its charmed urban shopfront in the chic heartland of Prenzlauer Berg.

Like the borough it calls home, No Fire No Glory has come of age: now a favourite brunch spot for the area's increasingly sophisticated – yet politically and socially conscious – denizens. Along with an impeccable, single-origin brew with steamed oatmilk, it is nigh on impossible to look past 'The Bomb': a Canadian-inspired pancake stack with organic poached egg, wafers of crisp bacon and coffee-infused maple syrup drizzled liberally. The menu also features vegan and vegetarian options, plus cold brews and premium filtered coffee: for those nostalgic for the Berlin of yesteryear (albeit with a gourmet touch). The terrace seats are in high demand in the warmer months, but the interior is equally inviting with plush sofas, original artwork and a cosy back room where you can while away the morning with a newspaper

Rykestrasse 45

Mon–Sun 9am–5pm

€5–15

28 83 92 33

nofirenoglory.de

Tram Marienburger Strasse

Sowohl Als Auch

*Geographically themed breakfast dishes and cakes
to write home about.*

Germans really love their cake and here you'll need to face up to one of life's most agonising decisions: baked peach and sour cream tart or hazelnut, almond and mascarpone torte infused with chocolate and amaretto? Once a winsome symbol of prosperity, today 'kuchen' (cake) is a certified national pastime: and no afternoon coffee is complete without a slice from the local 'konditorei' (artisan confectionery baker). And when it comes to cake few names loom larger than café Sowohl Als Auch – a cryptic local adage, loosely translating to 'as well as'. It's not uncommon to see customers perfectly bamboozled as they confront the multifarious cake selection.

Beyond the incandescent cake cabinet, Sowohl Als Auch also boasts one of the city's finest breakfast menus, with dishes brandishing names such as: Boston (eggs with tabasco and bread); Brandenburg (a selection of country hams, goat's cheese, tomato and fruits); Madrid (serrano, chorizo, Manchego and olives); Moscow (Russian pelmeni dumplings with sour cream and beetroot); Lyon (a broad cheese selection with fruits and bread); and London (sage derby, cheddar and sausages)   all representing the flavours of their name-of-origin. In honour of its working-class heritage, the Berliner breakfast is an honest-yet-satisfying plate of three fried eggs and dried ham on seeded dark bread, whilst the Oslo breakfast is laden with salmon, prawns and dill-infused cream, with lashing of caviar. It's all dished up in a quaint 19th century Vienna-style coffee house setting, replete with glistening chandeliers, yellow-washed walls, cosy furniture and ornate mirrors.

Kollwitzstrasse 88   Mon–Sun 8am–10pm   €7–15

442 93 11   tortenundkuchen.de

Tram Prenzlauer Allee/
Danziger Strasse

Geist Im Glas

Brunch haven by day, cocktail bar by night.

The supper club movement changed everything in Berlin during the noughties. Suddenly it seemed as though, overnight, everyone was en route to some secret bolthole with a mid-priced bottle of wine tucked under their arm (itself a revelation in a city that has a predilection for cheap booze), eyes aglow with furtive anticipation. Geist Im Glas was one such place: a bar that moonlighted as a gastronomic refuge for those craving something a little more exhilarating than processed pork. Then in 2016 fire brought the venue to ruins. Its British owner, Aishah Bennett, however, didn't give up and – after much restoration – reopened in 2017: now reinvented as a cocktail bar-cum-weekend brunch haven, bringing some supper club-style finesse to the morning breakfast table.

The Geist Im Glas pancake plate is something of folklore in Berlin and you have to try the impossibly fluffy buttermilk pancakes filled with banana and dished up with dulce de leche and – of course – a shot of bourbon maple syrup. There is also a Canadian pancake option laden with bacon and eggs. But beyond its signature dish, the menu has plenty to get excited about, including sweet and spicy waffles with chicken and a loaded plate of huevos rancheros – best paired with a Prince Harry: a mimosa cocktail with orange, herbs and an optional shot of bourbon. Start your day with a bang!

📍	🕧	€
Lenaustrasse 27	Mon–Fri 7am–2am	€9–15
	Sat–Sun 10am–2am	
📞		W
01 76 55 33 04 50		geist-im-glas.business.site
🚇		
U-Bahn Hermannplatz		

Roamers

A leading force behind Neukölln's café-culture renaissance.

Roamers is an intrepid pioneer of Berlin's brunch scene. It is much respected for its small yet bold menu: with a range of egg-centric (and occasionally eccentric) dishes, plus a swathe of plates that very much celebrate Berlin's geographic position in far northern Europe – including smoked salmon framed by horseradish, pickled radish, capers and poached egg, as well as glazed beetroot on bread with roasted hazelnut and marjoram. You can get a little wild with the Where the Wild Boars Roam plate: two fried eggs with forest honey, a regional wild boar sausage, bean stew, chimichurri, avocado and caper speckled feta.

It is festooned with planters, random bric-a-brac and artfully mismatched furniture. And it just wouldn't be the Neukölln kiez (neighbourhood), legendary for its bars and nightlife, without some morning libation, which comes in the form of a choice of dazzling breakfast cocktails like the Candy May: a sour gin with hibiscus, lemon, coriander and egg white.

📍 Pannierstrasse 64

🕐 Tues–Fri 9.30am–6pm
Sat–Sun 10am–6pm

€ €9–15

📞 01 76 55 33 04 50

W roamers.cc

🚇 U-Bahn Hermannplatz

Silo Coffee

*Australian-style contemporary cafe in gritty
former East Berlin.*

The borough of Friedrichshain has always guarded its unpolished authenticity. While the rest of the inner city exploded with trendy brunching eateries and organic juicing joints, this inner-city borough bordering the River Spree didn't flinch, maintaining its unique blend of down-to-earth eateries, small localised bars and bolthole artisan shops. Silo may have Australian origins but it wholly embraces Friedrichshain's autonomous spirit: eschewing Berlin's often uninspiring breakfast and brunch landscape to offer meals fit for the craftiest Melbourne laneway cafe.

Avocado on toast? Yes. Organic poached eggs? You bet. Soul-warming shakshuka. Indeed. House-crafted spiced sausages with white beans, minzu salad and a cider tomato dressing? We thought you'd never ask! With exposed brick and a handsome wood finish, this petite eatery also serves up rollicking good coffee and all your other mandatory morning requirements: namely Bloody Marys with lemon and a sprig of rosemary for salubrious measure. Australia (or New Zealand, depending on who you ask) may be the birthplace of the flat white–style coffee, but antipodean cafe culture has met its match in Berlin's eastern heartland.

📍	🕐	€
Gabriel-Max-Strasse 4	Mon–Fri 8.30am–5pm	€5–15
	Sat–Sun 9.30am–6pm	
🚋		W
Tram Simplonstrasse		silo-coffee.com

KaDeWe

Berlin's icon of 20th-century splendour reigns on.

Few institutions share such a symbiotic relationship with their city as the Kaufhaus des Westens (Department store of the West), better known as KaDeWe. While 'old world' may befit this haughty heirloom – often coined the 'Harrods of continental Europe' – it's not all pearls, snuff and caviar: with some of Berlin's most exciting gastronomic upstarts, such as BRLO's chicken and beer (see p.120) and Thai-fusion favourite Papaya Royal now nudging in beside the establishment to maintain KaDeWe's place as an essential stop on Berlin's gastronomic trail.

Beyond its floors of luxurious fashion brands and the chattels of haute couture, the KaDeWe is notorious for its 6th-floor delicatessen – a warren of laneways and nooks where oysters and champagne before noon are quite acceptable (even respectable) and where the senses are seduced by everything from bouillabaisse to hand-crafted bratwurst and kransky. Cult Israeli–Palestinian restaurant Kanaan (see p.123) has also brought its trademark flavours to the KaDeWe, dishing up exotic all-day twists such as the Oriental Plate with pilaf, chicken breast, linseed and grilled seasonal vegetables.

The history of this illustrious shrine to luxury and decadence is the story of Berlin itself: of imperial might, fin de siècle idealism, the ravages of war (a US bomber crash-landed on the building in 1943), the Nazi pogroms and the brutal quartering of the ruins of Berlin after World War II. The KaDeWe would eventually rise phoenix-like from the smouldering rubble to become the gaudy symbol of West Berlin and the 'free world': a glistening island of ostentatious luxury landlocked in an empire of communist austerity.

📍 Tauentzienstrasse 21–4

🕑 Mon–Thurs 10am–8pm
Fri 10am–9pm
Sat 9.30am–8pm

€ €10–30

📞 212 10

W kadewe.de

🚇 U-Bahn Wittenbergplatz

The Barn (Café Kranzler)

*Where old Berlin meets new in a truly
iconic location.*

Mention the name Café Kranzler and West Berliners are likely to get all misty-eyed. It may now host the city's finest roastery and be the most chic purveyor of coffee, but this café's pedigree goes back to 1825, when Austrian confectionery maestro Johann Georg Kranzler opened its doors on Unter den Linden (see p.85): a place where Berlin's polished classes would come to enjoy such rare and exotic luxuries as coffee and ice-cream. That building was lost to Allied bombs, but the Kranzler was resurrected in Charlottenburg – where it would become an emblem of West Germany's Wirtschaftswunder (German economic miracle), mainlined by the Marshall Plan. Its distinctive 1950s red-and-white striped canopy became a motif of indulgence – and its legend spread to East Berlin, where its otherworldly reputation was only rivalled by that of the KaDeWe (see p.59).

Somewhat ironically, the downfall of the East would spell Café Kranzler's eventual demise – as the epicentre of a newly reunified Berlin drifted back to Mitte, the physical centre of Berlin. Life, however, has finally returned to the historic rotunda as it also has to this once-booming commercial centre of Berlin's West, with The Barn setting up shop in this celebrated locale. Enjoy the city's best brews and house-made cakes and cookies with a 360-degree-views of the famous Kurfürstendamm avenue (see p.197), beneath the historic red-and-white awnings.

Kurfürstendamm 18	Mon–Sun 10am–8pm	€15–15
U-Bahn Kurfürstendamm		thebarn.de

MARS

A former crematorium now cooking up breakfasts to die for.

📍

Gerichtstrasse 35

📞

01 20 82 21 50

🚆

U-Bahn Leopoldplatz,
S-Bahn Wedding

🕐

Mon–Fri 12pm–6pm
Sat–Sun 10am–5pm

€

€7–15

W

mars-berlin.net

What do you do with a decommissioned heritage-listed crematorium? In edgy Berlin, turn it into a restaurant of course. In just a few short years Silent Green – as the complex has now become known – has become an electrifying hub of art and gastronomy, with regular pop-up events and restaurants in the circular chapel room, ornate balconies and domed roof, and permanent on-site eatery, MARS.

Whilst the kitchen serves up simple fare to lunch crowds each weekday, it's on the weekend that the place begins to sizzle as those in the know flock to enjoy one of Berlin's finest brunch menus: featuring everything from shakshuka to Belgian waffles and the fabled Silent Green breakfast plate with raw milk cheeses, house-made sausages and fresh garden vegetables with lashings of pesto. Inside, the walls are plastered with retro wallpaper, but the terraced area is most inviting, with the wooden tables shaded beneath dense foliage.

Mirage Bistrot

A cafe that embraces Wedding's history as Berlin's 'French sector'.

Reinickendorferstrasse 110

46 99 20 74

S-Bahn Wedding

Tues–Wed 10am–8pm
Thurs–Fri 10am–10pm
Sat–Sun 10am–6pm

€2–9

W

mirage.berlin

After World War II, the borough of Wedding fell to the French. After reunification, however, this once frontier borough quietly drifted into dormancy but is now gloriously rousing from its deep slumber. Mirage Bistrot's bold gamble to set up shop in this once weathered hood lined with kebab joints has paid off – and today people travel from all over Berlin to enjoy its all-day breakfasts and legendary weekend brunch.

Come here for soul-nourishing classics like croque chèvre, French toast with banana and chocolate or eggs benedict. Verdant planters lend an exotic feel to the room, illuminated by large windows and charmed pendant lighting: all complemented by bright furnishings, which add a playful touch. In the afternoon the light, airy space transforms into an Alsatian-style bistro with a range of tartes flambées to pair with a carafe of sauvignon blanc.

Mana

*Berlin's benchmark vegan eatery for morning and
night, set in the elegant surrounds of Schöneberg.*

Back when the Berlin Wall still cleaved this city in two, Schöneberger kiez,
an aesthetically blessed neighbourhood of West Berlin, was forging on with
a radical social agenda: emerging as the spiritual home of Berlin's gay and
lesbian community, a centre of art and free expression and also one of the
city's most progressive culinary landscapes. The frontiers may have been
redrawn since those heady days, when the likes of David Bowie and Nick
Cave haunted the cobbled laneways, but Schöneberg maintains its dynamic
disposition: with eateries like Mana continuing to rewrite the rulebook.

While the Mana vegan bowls and brunch are blockbusters, it's the
burgers that are killing the pig ... well, metaphorically speaking (yes, in Berlin
anything goes ... even vegan burgers for brunch). The black bean burger
packs a toothsome punch with a 'meaty' bean patty, jalapenos, vegan cheese
and salad, with Mana's trademark burger sauce. And the tandoori burger –
generously loaded with a linseed and quinoa patty with wasabi, cabbage,
sun-dried tomatoes and pea-mint paste – is a revelation (especially when
paired with the morning booster beetroot milk: beetroot juice with coconut
and oat milk). In the unique spirit of this kiez, Mana sources its kombucha,
beer and even its mineral water from producers all within walking distance
of the restaurant. The minimalist aesthetic – with Scandinavian-style
furnishings, tea light candles and exposed brick – is the perfect blank canvas
for the generous and playful light that floods in through the windows and
arched doorway.

Belziger Strasse 34	Mon–Sat 10am–11pm	€5–15
	Sun 10am–4pm	
23 53 00 32		mana-food.de
U-Bahn Eisenacher Strasse		

MITTAGS

– noon –

Berlin by day means a day on foot amidst museums and headline historic sites. Berlin's story is largely defined by the 19th and 20th centuries: with visitors naturally curious in exploring spaces related to the city's Nazi history and the Berlin Wall. The city is pockmarked with such places to experience: amongst them sections of the Wall, including East Side Gallery (see p.95) – with its iconic graffiti art – and Berlin Wall Memorial and Documentation Centre (see p.93). When it comes to the tragedies of World War II, the Berlin authorities have gone to great lengths to acknowledge the city's troubled past. Key sites include the sobering Memorial to the Murdered Jews of Europe (see p.77) and the Topography of Terror (see p.71), with its confronting exploration of Berlin's darkest days. If you're more interested in Berlin's imperial history, the city also offers a glimpse into its regal past as the seat of the Hohenzollern dynasty: replete with ample palaces, churches and historic monuments, including the UNESCO-listed Museum Island (see p.69), with its reconstructed Berlin City Palace and world-renowned Pergamon Museum.

Museum Island

*A tiny isle in the River Spree with serious
headline attractions.*

This small archipelago has some of the city's most significant museums
and galleries: the Bode-Museum (medieval and Byzantine sculpture),
Neues Museum (classical antiquities, Egyptian and pre-history, including
the enigmatic bust of Queen Nefertiti), Alte Nationalgalerie (paintings
from Romanticism through to Impressionism and early Modernism), Altes
Museum (sculptures of antiquity) and the Pergamon Museum (Ishtar Gates,
Pergamon Altar and many works of Islamic antiquity). It's impossible to see
everything in a day, so choose a few and do them well. The Pergamon and
Alte Nationalgalerie never fail to dazzle.

Museum Island is also an exceptional site in its own right: the
UNESCO listed location of the long-erased Berlin City Palace (Stadtschloss)
and later East German parliament, the Palace of the Republic, demolished at
the very same site in 2008. The islands enduring examples of neoclassical
architecture are complemented by the imposing Berliner Dom (cathedral),
built in 1905. The Fischerinsel (Fisher's Island at the southern tip of the
island, dating back to 1237) is the site of Cölln, one of the city's two original
settlements. The charming Lustgarten square was centre stage for Prussian
military might under Friedrich Wilhelm I, and Adolf Hitler delivered some of his
most decisive speeches here. In an unexpected twist of history, the Berlin City
Palace – once the royal seat of power – has been rebuilt as an ethnological
museum and gallery of Asian art.

Tickets are €18 (€9 concession) and will give you one-day access to all
the museums and galleries on the island.

📍	🕑	€
Am Lustgarten 1	Fri–Wed 10am–6pm	€18/9
	Thurs 10am–8pm	
📞		W
266 424 242		smb.museum
🚈		
S-Bahn Hackescher Markt		

Topography of Terror

*Chronology of Nazi crimes on the site of the Gestapo
and SS headquarters.*

Nothing here makes for a 'pleasant' visit. The frank, visceral and often distressing accounts document the narrative arc of Nazi systematic terror: from planning to execution. Once the ominous site of the Nazi's secret police and much feared SS constabulary – adjacent to the former office of Hermann Göring and his Luftwaffe (now Detlev-Rohwedder-Haus, which survived the war) – the Topography of Terror features two permanent exhibitions detailing Germany's darkest days.

The external exhibition runs alongside the remnants of the Berlin Wall – the lengthiest section of outer Wall remaining – and charts the rise of the Nazis during the Weimar era (1918–33). It also reveals excavations of the physical remains of the Gestapo and SS command centre: an abyss of interrogation and torture. The second permanent exhibition – housed in a sober building designed by Ursula Wilms and opened in 2010 – traces the many crimes engineered and often executed here at this very site, largely through archival photographs. Allow at least two hours for your visit.

The Topography of Terror sits in the shadow of the Martin-Gropius-Bau: a handsome exhibition space – and welcome change of perspective – built by Martin Gropius (the great uncle of Walter Gropius, who founded the Bauhaus School of architecture and design). The grandiose Abgeordnetenhaus across the road is the home of the Berlin state legislature, dating back to Prussian rule.

📍	🕐	€
Niederkirchnerstrasse 8	Mon–Sun 10am–8pm	Free
📞		W
25 45 09 50		topographie.de
🚌		
U-Bahn Kochstrasse/ Checkpoint Charlie		

Reichstag

*The seat of German parliament, and the site
of Adolf Hitler's 1933 power grab.*

Few buildings symbolise the hope and desperation of Berlin quite as potently as the Reichstag; and standing in its forecourt it's impossible not to feel the palpable weight of modern history. The unification of Germany in 1871 ushered in a golden age for Berlin as the capital of the German Empire: with Wilhelm I its emperor and the Reichstag, constructed in 1894, the seat of a people's national parliament.

Following World War I, the Weimar era (1918–33) saw parliamentary democracy flourish: a sentiment manifested in a bold inscription added to the building in 1916 and clearly visible today, reading: 'Dem Deutschen Volke' (For The German People). Severe economic depression and the war reparations of the 1919 *Treaty of Versailles* arguably fuelled the rise of Adolf Hitler and his Nazi party, who exploited a catastrophic fire in the building on 27 February 1933 to seize emergency powers through the *Enabling Act* and suppress all rivals. The building lay in ruins for decades and only barely escaped razing – with the Norman Foster-imagined reconstruction (replete with a grand glass dome) finally opening in 1999 as the federal seat of a reunified Germany. Today you're welcome to explore the glass dome, featuring a historic photo exhibition and stunning vistas. Gerhard Richter's *Birkenau Suite* of abstract paintings adorn the entrance hall of the Reichstag as a poignant reminder of the Holocaust.

You must register online before visiting.

📍
Platz der Republik 1

📞
22 62 99 33

🚌
S + U-Bahn
Brandenburger Tor

🕐
Mon–Sun 8am–12am

€
Free, with prior
online registration

W
bundestag.de

Hackesche Höfe

Resplendent Art Nouveau courtyards capturing
Prussian grandeur.

The Hackesche Höfe stands as an emblem of the remarkable period of innovation and progress that defined the Wilhelmine era (1888–1918): a time of great social and artistic progress in Germany, which has largely been historically overshadowed by the post-World War I Weimar era (1918–33) that followed it. In his 1905 love declaration to Berlin, *The Beauty of the Metropolis*, August Endell wrote of the time period: 'Only fools and weaklings seek a golden age either before or after their own.' The Wilhelmine era would prove a harbinger of the Berlin we know and celebrate today.

Completed in 1906, the Hackesche Höfe is Endell's paean to Prussian beauty and 'Heimat': a mercurial word that translates to something between 'homeland', 'belonging' and 'ancestry'. The Jugendstil (Art Nouveau) facades to the interconnected courtyards are rendered with ornate ceramic tiles coloured white, green and blue: an aesthetic hotchpotch falling between Portuguese Azulejo and Prussian Gothic, and highly worthy of a half-hour stroll. Make sure to look up! Today the area mainly houses a famed restaurant (see p.39), a cinema, cabaret theatre and retail – including the original Ampelmann Shop, celebrating East Berlin's iconic hatted pedestrian traffic symbol. However, the area was long home to a vibrant Jewish community, which would worship at the Alhambra-inspired New Synagogue on Oranienburger Strasse nearby. The synagogue has now been fully restored.

📍
Rosenthaler Strasse 40–1

🕐
Mon–Fri 8am–12am
Sat–Sun 9am–12am

€
Free

🚊
S-Bahn Hackescher Markt

W
hackesche-hoefe.de

Mittags

Memorial to the Murdered Jews of Europe

Interpretive monument to Germany's darkest chapter.

Architect Peter Eisenman's memorial to the Holocaust sits on 19,000 square metres (over four acres), between the Brandenburg Gate (see p.87) and Potsdamer Platz (see p.91). It features thousands of grey, austere concrete pillars and an underground information centre. The Holocaust remains one of history's most heinous crimes – two thirds of Europe's Jewish population murdered in such systematic fashion that it continues to challenge the very essence of civilised humanity. The meaning behind the pillars here remain open to interpretation: for many resembling tombstones and for others presenting distortions on perspective, which often finds visitors feeling imprisoned amidst the towering pillars. It is a truly moving site and, when partnered with the below-ground information centre, takes around an hour to navigate.

The site of Hitler's 'Führerbunker', where he hid out the final days of the war and eventually committed suicide, can be found nearby (in den Ministergärten), buried beneath a carpark with a simple and unembellished informational panel (to avoid it becoming a shrine to Nazi sympathisers). Nearby in the Tiergarten (see p.201) stand separate memorials to the homosexual and Sinti and Roma victims of National Socialism.

📍
Cora-Berliner-Strasse 1

📞
263 94 30

🚇
S + U-Bahn
Brandenburger Tor

🕐
Memorial 24 hours /
Information Centre
Tues–Sun 10am–7pm

€
Free

W
stiftung-denkmal.de

Hamburger Bahnhof

*Temple to contemporary art in a palatial
19th-century train station.*

If World War II left Germany brutalised by bombs and destroyed by ideology, it left its artists in a bottomless existential void – a chaotic yet vital period of cultural expression, of which a great deal is housed in one of Germany's oldest train stations of the neoclassical period.

Artist Joseph Beuys had come of age in the Hitler Youth and fought for the Luftwaffe before re-emerging as a chief agitator in the post-war Fluxus movement of the 1960s and '70s: forging cryptic conceptual works that upended art, politics and history through intermedia and multi-form experimentation. Along with contemporaries such as Gerhard Richter, Sigmar Polke, Imi Knoebel and A. R. Penck, Beuys' work – including the 1983 'ruined' installation *The End of the Twentieth Century* – reacted to a country rattled by trauma, guilt and renewal. Beuys' works can be explored in the west wing.

The imposing building features works from the 1960s onwards, including international artists such as Andy Warhol, Jeff Koons, Robert Rauschenberg and Cy Twombly. Many of these can be found in the historic hall and Kleihueshalle of the old railway station as part of the Sammlung Marx collection. The overall collection – easily worthy of an entire morning or afternoon – enjoys a reputation akin to the Tate Modern in London, and a visit is often paired with the nearby Natural History Museum to create an entire day's experience.

📍
Invalidenstrasse 50–1

📞
266 42 42 42

🚆
S + U-Bahn Berlin
Hauptbahnhof

🕑
Tues–Wed & Fri
10am–6pm
Sat–Sun 11am–6pm
Thurs 10am–8pm

€
€7/14

W
smb.museum

Alexanderplatz

*The heartland of Berlin hedonism later reimagined
as a worker's utopia.*

Berlin's largest square and a busy transport hub, Alexanderplatz once represented Berlin's lascivious side with its scurrilous lust for life. During the 1920s, Alexanderplatz became an epicentre of Berlin's many countercultures of the Weimar era (1918–33), replete with garish neon light – a seedier cousin of Potsdamer Platz (see p.91). Alfred Döblin's 1929 novel *Berlin Alexanderplatz* (see p.221) invites the reader into this unbridled and often furtive side of the city: a not-always-so 'Golden '20s' of jazz, crime, drugs, prostitution and sexual liberation.

World War II left Alexanderplatz smouldering – its soul wrenched out along with the statue of *Berolina*, the city's iron symbol. The East Germans redeveloped the site as a showpiece of German socialism: a pedestrian and transport zone with sweeping avenues still lined with aweing examples of socialist neoclassical architecture with hints of brutalism, centered around the city's most omnipresent landmark: the Fernsehturm (TV Tower), the tallest structure in Germany. Today Alexanderplatz is a busy train and tram terminus and commercial centre with offices, department stores and hotels – with Soviet-era haunts offering a glimpse into life in the German Democratic Republic, including the Kino International on Karl-Marx-Allee (formerly Stalinallee), where General Secretary Erich Honecker reputedly came to unwind. As well as admiring the imposing Soviet architecture or having a spot of department store therapy, Alexanderplatz is the perfect jumping-off point to explore the Nikolaiviertel (see p.83): Berlin's oldest quarter.

Alexanderplatz

S + U-Bahn
Alexanderplatz

Nikolaiviertel
(Nikolai Quarter)

*Berlin's ancient quarter, given a Cold War
pre-fab makeover.*

Long before its rise as an epicurean city, Berlin was a sleepy medieval village set on marshland in the chilly far reaches of northern Europe – just across the River Spree from the neighbouring settlement of Cölln. Little survives of these old towns today: abandoned as rubble after World War II, until Berlin's 750th anniversary in 1987, when the East German authorities resurrected the old town of Berlin – albeit not of stone but Plattenbau (prefabricated concrete). While the area has a hint of 'film set recreation' about it, it nevertheless maintains a discernibly historical demeanour: serpentine cobbled lanes framed with cafes and cosy German eateries that wrap around the recreated Nikolaikirche (Nikolai Church), which is now a museum dedicated to the area's rich history. Venture down the main street Poststrasse and onto Propststrasse.

Although geographically in the centre of the city and ever popular with tourists (especially domestic ones), Nikolaiviertel enjoys a sense of village quietude with poky laneways and small shops – including antique dealers and even an old-fashioned hat shop – but also a plethora of souvenir and trinket haunts of the sort you'd expect to find in such a historic and popular locale (faux medieval ceramic stein mug anyone?). The 13th-century Marienkirche (St Mary's Church) suffered a less catastrophic fate during the war and is today the city's oldest surviving church – its vestibule adorned with the faded and enigmatic *Totentanz (Dance of Death)* mural.

♀
Nikolaikirchplatz

🚃
U-Bahn Klosterstrasse,
S + U-Bahn
Alexanderplatz

W
berlin-nikolaiviertel.com

Mittags

Unter den Linden

*Berlin's most celebrated boulevard – oft celebrated
in stories, cinema and song.*

Johann Strauss III wrote a waltz dedicated to it; Christopher Isherwood (see p.221) set some of *Goodbye to Berlin*'s headiest scenes in its most famous hotel; and, of course, Marlene Dietrich (see p.220) sang tributes to the fabled boulevard. Indeed, this 1.5 kilometre (0.9 miles) stretch of asphalt has been a beacon to visitors for centuries. Once a 16th-century bridle path connecting the Berlin City Palace (see p.69) to the Tiergarten (the royal family's hunting playground, see p.201), it flourished with the metropolis, becoming the central nervous system that connected the Berlin City Palace and Museum Island (see p.69) with the Brandenburg Gate (see p.87).

In between these two geographical bookends lie some of Berlin's most significant sites, including the German Historical Museum: an all-encompassing museum on German history from its ancient roots through to today, housed in the oldest surviving building on the boulevard: the Zeughaus. While the star-studded boulevard has too many historic sites to list, highlights include the Neue Wache memorial, a small former Prussian guardhouse featuring artist Käthe Kollwitz' moving sculpture *Pietá*, known as *Mother with Dead Son*; and Bebelplatz, the site of the most notorious Nazi book burning ceremony, where 20,000 works of 'degenerate' poetry, philosophy and Jewish literature were torched in 1933. It's now the site of a subterranean memorial featuring empty bookshelves. The storied Hotel Adlon (see p.113) at Pariser Platz and the nearby Brandenburg Gate (see p.87) occupy its western reaches.

📍

Unter den Linden

🚌

S + U-Bahn
Brandenburger Tor,
S + U-Bahn
Friedrichstrasse

Brandenburg Gate

*The city's most recognisable landmark, and once
the Cold War frontier between East and West.*

As a relatively young city compared with other European capitals, Berlin's
illustrious line of monarchs and architects have often channelled aesthetic
Grecian and Roman classicism in the hope of it lending the German capital
a dose of historical and mythical weight. While originally little more than a
custom's checkpoint – one of 18 eventually constructed in the 18th century –
'Brandenburger Tor' could have been cut from the Acropolis, with its
Corinthian columns adorned with a sculpture of a quadriga with the goddess
Victoria astride. Completed in 1791 the gate eventually became a site of regal
procession – something exploited by Napoleon Bonaparte, who paraded his
temporary triumph over Prussia through the gate in 1806 ... before ordering
the crowning sculpture be dismantled and carted back to Paris.

   The Prussians returned the sentiment in 1814, seizing Paris and
reclaiming the sculpture: restoring it to its rightful place, with an iron cross
added for additional providence. Brandenburg Gate sat centre stage through
the tumult of the 20th century: from the rise of Hitler to the quartering of
the city, where it formed a barrier between East and West. US Presidents
Kennedy and Reagan both advocated for reconciliation here, but it would
be another American – conductor Leonard Bernstein – who would claim the
collective hearts at this very site following the collapse of the Wall in 1989,
leading the Berlin Philharmonic Orchestra in Beethoven's *Ode to Joy*, which
he remodelled as *Ode to Freedom*.

Pariser Platz

S + U-Bahn
Brandenburger Tor

Gendarmenmarkt

*Beguiling 18th-century city square and pivotal
site of Reformation history.*

Berlin's most handsome square is home to several grand buildings, such as
the Konzerthaus (concert hall) and Französischer Dom (French Cathedral),
constructed between 1701–5. The Reformation began in Germany under Martin
Luther, and In France the Huguenot peoples answered the call but Louis
XIV's *Edict of Fontainebleau* of 1685 spelled a gloomy fate for them. Many
Huguenots fled, including 20,000 to Berlin where Prussian ruler Friedrich
Wilhelm had promised safe-haven under the *Edict of Potsdam* – continuing
Berlin's long tradition as a place of refuge. Gendarmenmarkt was named for
the Huguenot Gens d'Armes.

  The Französischer Dom today stands as testament to this act of
mercy and houses the Huguenot Museum, which is a fascinating insight
into the Huguenot story, complemented by the German Church on the other
flank of the square, built in tandem. The neo-classical Konzerthaus (opened
in 1821) – designed by Prussia's most celebrated architect Karl Friedrich
Schinkel, also responsible for the Altes Museum and Neue Wache Memorial
(see p.85), as well as early set designs for Mozart's *The Magic Flute* –
completes the resplendent panorama. Today it hosts a range of classical music
concerts; and enjoying a classical performance from the German repertoire
inside this imposing building is a highlight of any visit to Berlin. Painstakingly
restored after World War II, the square also hosts the city's most picturesque
Christmas Market (see p.181) each December.

%

Gendarmenmarkt

gendarmenmarkt.de

U-Bahn Stadtmitte

Potsdamer Platz

Once Europe's busiest traffic intersection,
this symbolic quarter has risen from the ashes.

To the casual eye there's little to this patch, situated just two kilometres to the south-west of the city's thumping heart of Mitte – a contemporary business district that can feel a little kitsch. But looks can deceive, and the area is a major tourist drawcard for its shopping malls, the State library, cinemas and that perennial favourite: Legoland. Dating back to the Middle Ages, Potsdamer Platz was one of Prussia's main toll gates. As Berlin emerged in the late 19th century as the world's most populous metropolis after New York and London, Potsdamer Platz's legend was cast: luxurious villas, resplendent department stores, gilded embassies, merchants of finery and – most infamously – cabaret clubs, such as the 'pleasure palace' of Haus Vaterland.

Potsdamer Platz was obliterated by Allied battery on 26 February 1945, and the ascent of the Berlin Wall furthered its grim fate – leaving it a tumbleweed wasteland and rendering its once bustling S-Bahn train station (one of Europe's busiest) a Geisterbahnhof (ghost station). Following reunification in 1990, Potsdamer Platz began to rise once again and today is a contemporary shopping, commercial and entertainment hub – and also home to the Berlinale Film Festival (a must-see if visiting in February), Philharmonie (the headquarters of globally distinguished Berlin Philharmonic Orchestra) and Neue Nationalgalerie, featuring early 20th-century art.

📍

Corner Ebertstrasse and
Potsdamer Strasse

🚋

S + U-Bahn Potsdamer
Platz

W

potsdamerplatz.de

Berlin Wall Memorial and Documentation Centre

*The most stirring reminder of the Wall that divided
a city and its people.*

On 22 August 1961, Ida Siekmann plunged from her fourth-storey window on Bernauer Strasse in a bid to escape to West Berlin, just metres below. Her desperate flight would tragically herald the first casualty of the Berlin Wall – a sombre distinction, which would be followed by many others who perished trying to breach the border, with some putting estimates on the death toll as high as 239.

Bernauer Strasse had long been a flashpoint street between East and West – the proximity between both sides made this a pivotal vantage point for more daring escape methods, including tunnels that criss-crossed the subterranean. The most notorious was Tunnel 57, which in 1964 enabled that number of East Germans to escape during a two-night operation that saw a border guard killed. The stretch of Wall that stands here today – as well as the engaging Wall Documentation Centre, directly opposite – is a stirring place of reflection, with detailed information panels marking the street's tumultuous Cold War history, as well as rare moments of hope, including the iconic photograph of East German soldier Hans Konrad Schumann caught mid-flight leaping across the barbed wire as he made his daring and successful dash to freedom in 1961.

◉	**◷**	**€**
Bernauer Strasse 111	Wall Memorial	Free
	Mon–Sun 24-hours	
☎	Documentation Centre	**W**
467 98 66 66	Mon 10am–4pm	berliner-mauer-
	Tues–Sun 10am–6pm	gedenkstaette.de
🚆		
S-Bahn Nordbahnhof		

East Side Gallery

*The most iconic stretch of Berlin Wall, plastered
in graffitied artwork.*

Although Friedrichshain and Kreuzberg – separated by the River Spree –
are today a united administrative borough, until 1989 the two suburbs were
separated by not only water but a 3.6 metre (11 foot) wall of concrete and
heavily armed guard towers. Today the 1.3 kilometre (0.8 miles) stretch of
remaining Wall has become a potent symbol of a city now united. Perhaps
Berlin's most photographed landmark after the Reichstag (see p.73),
Brandenburg Gate (see p.87) and TV Tower (see p.81), the East Side Gallery
was transformed into the world's longest open-air art gallery in 1990 (the
official year of reunification). In 1990 artists from around the globe inked 105
paintings onto its austere concrete facade, including iconic images such as
the notorious 'fraternal kiss' between Soviet leader Leonid Brezhnev and East
German leader Erich Honecker, by Dmitri Vrubel.

Another often photographed image is Birgit Kinder's portrait of
a Trabant (aka, the 'Trabi'), East Germany's distinctive 'people's car',
manufactured from 1967–1990, breaking through the Wall. As an aside,
budget models of the vehicle famously had no headlights nor speedometer,
and no fuel gauge nor fuel door, with petrol administered directly beneath
the hood. The car was decommissioned in 1991, although there are plans to
reintroduce the emblematic Trabant as an electric vehicle.

Many of the paintings have recently been restored due to deterioration
and wanton graffiti. The site is accessible 24/7.

📍	🕐	W
Mühlenstrasse 1	Mon–Sun 24-hours	eastsidegallery-berlin.com
🚋		
S-Bahn Ostbahnhof		

Kaiser Wilhelm Memorial Church

Church ruins that remain as an ever-present
memory of the brutality of war.

For a man whose architecture was once synonymous with the city, little remains of Architect Franz Heinrich Schwechten's legacy in Berlin. A student of Martin Gropius, Schwechten came into his own infamy with the Prussian Military Academy (1883), Romanesque House (1901) and Haus Vaterland pleasure palace in Potsdamer Platz (1912, see p.91) – all later expunged from the landscape by war. His landmark Anhaller Bahnhof train station – once the grandest in continental Europe – later became the ominous deportation point for 55,000 Berlin Jews to the concentration camps of central and eastern Europe, and today only the facade remains as a solemn memorial to its pivotal place in the Holocaust.

Schwechten's Kaiser Wilhelm Memorial Church (1891) in Charlottenburg would also suffer Allied bombardment, albeit with the fractured spire and front hall remaining largely intact at the close of the war. The battered remnants were preserved and today remain as a stark reminder of both hubris and the horrors of war; the internal floor mosaic of the Archangel Michael battling the dragon a powerful symbol of good's sometimes seemingly impossible battle against evil. A contemporary new church was constructed on the ruined section of the building, notable for its stark contrast of blue-stained glass set in ascetic concrete.

📍 Breitscheidplatz

🕐 Mon–Sun 9am–7pm

€ Free

📞 218 50 23

W gedaechtniskirche-berlin.de

🚇 U-Bahn Kurfürstendamm,
S + U-Bahn Zoologischer Garten

Brücke Museum

*A gallery dedicated to Germany's leading
Expressionist painters.*

This modest yet significant collection celebrates one of the most decisive moments in German art: German Expressionism, which had global implications. In cinema, the landmark works of Fritz Lang – such as *Metropolis* (1927), shot at the historic Babelsberg Film Studio on the outskirts of Berlin – would create a new and confrontational language for cinema that continues to resonate today. Painting in this new form, pioneered in Berlin, would channel the existential calamity of World War I to create an avant-garde form of visual language in stark contrast to the indulgent splendour of Impressionism, with an often-confronting rawness that informed the subsequent Weimar era (1918–33).

The Die Brücke (The Bridge) movement was a select group of German artists working in this radical new form, founded by Erich Heckel, Fritz Bleyl, Ernst Ludwig Kirchner and Karl Schmidt-Rottluff. This museum is located in Dahlem – a green idyll in south-west Berlin nearby Grunewald lake, with its historic hunting lodge and known for its 19th-century handsome villas. Although Die Brücke only lasted from 1905–13, the work of these artists would go on to influence all that followed, despite being classified as 'Entartete Kunst' (degenerate art), by the Nazi Party. The collection is exhibited in revolving themed exhibitions, including artworks in protest of the Nazi rise to power.

📍 Bussardsteig 9

🕟 Wed–Mon 11am–5pm

€ €5/8

📞 83 90 08 60

W bruecke-museum.de

🚌 Bus Clayallee/
Pücklerstrasse

Köpenick

*One of Berlin's oldest surviving settlements,
including a baroque palace.*

While little remains of Berlin's ancient foundations, Köpenick retains its ancient village-like allure: a virtual island hemmed in at the confluence of the Dahme and Spree rivers, and the winsome Müggelsee lake to the east.

Köpenick was founded in the 12th century during the Slavonic reign, becoming a leading seat of power to rival both Berlin and Cölln (see p.83). The historic Rathaus (Town Hall) commands the most attention, with its ornate Prussian brick facade and extensive vaulted cellar; it can be visited free of charge and is home to a fine regional restaurant.

Köpenick is also the scene of one of Berlin's most enduring folk tales: where, in 1906, a rapscallion swindler named Wilhelm Voigt relieved the treasury coffers of 4002 marks and 37 pfennigs (no small fortune). His heist became folklore, and a statue of the 'Captain of Köpenick' now guards the town hall doors. The 16th-century Köpenick Palace – once the hunting lodge of Joachim II, Elector of Brandenburg, and built on the site of an ancient Slavic fortress – keeps sentry from a small island in the Dahme River and is today the home of the Museum of Decorative Arts (€3/6 tickets), which features examples of interior design dating between the 16th and 18th centuries, including furniture, tapestries, mirrors, clocks and even wallpaper.

Schlossinsel 1

Tram Schlossplatz
Köpenick

Mittags

Zitadelle Spandau

Berlin's original fortress and oldest building,
keeping sentry over historic Spandau.

Zitadelle Spandau is an aweing legacy of Berlin's ancient history – an imposing citadel at the confluence of the rivers Havel and Spree that has stood, in various guises, since medieval times. While the Zitadelle has the dubious legacy of housing Germany's chemical warfare research headquarters in the late 1930s, today it is best known for its summer open-air concerts (that range from classical to rock and jazz – see its website). It is best visited in conjunction with the nearby and charmed Altstadt Spandau, or Old Town, which also hosts one of the city's most endearing Christmas markets (see p.181) in December. You can easily while away half a day strolling the citadel with its surrounding historic quarter, with the latter's striking Hanseatic-style architecture and bucolic riverside vistas.

After eventually wrestling control of the region from the rival Saxons, Bohemians and Slavic Wends, the Zitadelle Spandau was one of Albert the Bear's first major civic building projects in 1150: coveted for its hillside vantage encircled by protective waterways. The Hohenzollerns later remodelled the Zitadelle Spandau as a heavily fortified Renaissance military garrison in the mid-16th century and restored it yet again after wrestling it back from Napoleon's troops in 1813.

A self-guided visit through the expansive citadel takes around two hours. Be sure to scale to the top of the turret for some of Berlin's most commanding views, and the on-site museum houses a fascinating collection of paraphernalia including weapons, maps and models.

Am Juliusturm 64	Fri–Wed 10am–5pm Thurs 1–8pm	€2.50/4.50
354 94 40		zitadelle-berlin.de
U-Bahn Zitadelle		

Sanssouci Palace

*The 'Versailles of Berlin', albeit with a distinctly
Prussian aesthetic.*

While not formally part of Berlin, the city's history is indelibly linked to this palace at the end of the suburban train line in Potsdam: just two kilometres (1.2 miles) beyond the official periphery of Berlin. While most Berliners feel little nostalgia for the Hohenzollern reign – with most blaming Emperor Wilhelm II (1888–1918) for wrenching Germany into a first war that would inevitably beget a second – there remains a muted respect for Friedrich II, colloquially known as Friedrich the Great. While Der Alte Fritz's (the old Fritz's) rule over the Kingdom of Prussia is remembered for its military triumphs, it is equally remembered for its embrace of the Enlightenment: he was a patron of the arts, sciences and architecture.

Constructed between 1745–1747, Sanssouci – meaning 'without worry' – is a single-storey villa designed in a Rococo (late Baroque) style that reveals a great deal about Prussian power and its preference for a more modest aesthetic than its French and Austrian counterparts, albeit generously festooned with stucco and gilded appointments. A significant feature remains the ornate Picture Gallery, where Friedrich hung his favourite works of art, and the expansive terraced gardens, which also feature a Chinese Teahouse, 18th-century windmill and the much more ostentatious Baroque-style New Palace.

Any visit should be combined with a stroll through central Potsdam, with its enchanting Dutch and Russian quarters.

📍
Maulbeerallee, Potsdam

🕑
Tues–Sun 10am–5.30pm

€
€16/21

📞
19 69 42 00

W
spsg.de

🚌
S-Bahn Potsdam
Hauptbahnhof

ABENDS

– evening –

It's evening … it's dinner time. Gone are the boiled meats and lukewarm beer, which were once an enduring hallmark of Berlin's cuisine. The huge influx of international inhabitants in the early 21st century literally shook the city's culinary identity to the core, and today it's a true melting pot of flavour and flair – from street eats to the Michelin-star splendour of Pauly Saal (see p.111). The city's large Turkish population have played a boundless role in spicing up the Berliner table … inventing the world-conquering döner kebab in the process: of which Doyum Restaurant (see p.117) reigns supreme. Alt Berlin (Old Berlin) cuisine is staging an impressive comeback at places such as Max und Moritz (see p.119), with restaurants championing local and bio ingredients, thanks to the verdant fields and forests of Brandenburg, ripe with wild game (boar, dear, duck and rabbit) and endemic delicacies (white asparagus, forest berries, chestnuts and mushrooms). Marjellchen (see p.132) truly rouses a regional appetite. Yet the city also sizzles at the cutting edge of gastronomy, with Katz Orange (see p.115) at the coalface. And no day is truly complete without a currywurst: a Berlin icon, available (with a haughty twist) at Hotel Adlon (see p.113).

Lokal

*This once loveable lunch joint has now turned
up the heat in the evening.*

Lokal finds itself at the centre of Linienstrasse which, along with nearby Auguststrasse, has emerged as two of Berlin's most sophisticated thoroughfares in recent years – packed cheek-to-jowl with small private art galleries and boutiques. Lokal's minimal aesthetic fits right in, resembling a gallery itself, but with the paintings yet to be hung. Naturally, however, it is not the walls patrons are flocking to appreciate, but the small wooden tables adorned with some of Berlin's most exciting dishes.

As its name promises, Lokal is all about celebrating ingredients from Berlin and its Brandenburg surrounds, with an eye to sustainability: which on any given day could feature Brandenburg entrecote with wild broccoli, corn, forest mushrooms and gooseberry or a grilled backstrap of rabbit in a corn crepe with turnip and freshly plucked strawberries. Local game, such as wild boar, deer, pigeon and Brandenburg's famously succulent duck feature heavily alongside innovative vegetarian dishes that dare to pair local gherkin with spring rhubarb, carrot, estragon, sheep's cheese and freshly rolled noodles.

Book ahead for dinner and pair the evening with a gallery-hop down the ever-alluring Linienstrasse.

Linienstrasse 160

Mon–Sun 5pm–1am

€15–29

028 44 95 00

lokal-berlin.blogspot.com

Tram Tucholskystrasse

Pauly Saal

*With a Michelin nod, this fine eatery is where
Berlin's past and present collide perfectly.*

The opening of Pauly Saal in 2012 was a watershed moment: an unapologetic reclamation of a sophisticated Berlin dining culture that reaches back centuries, to when the city was a global centre of merchants, courtiers and kings. It was also the reclamation of history: a former Jewish girls school restored, and now also home to a museum and art gallery. Set on Auguststrasse – a strip famed for its boutique art galleries – Pauly Saal is a sanctuary of refinement. Any reservations you might have that the bar room resembles a stuffy gentlemen's club – replete with Chesterfield sofas and lavish Persian rugs – are quickly allayed on eyeing the 'Disco Longdrink' cocktail menu, where sake is weaved together with pear and bergamot syrup, lime and soda. Then there are the 600 or so international wines to choose from.

Inside the austere yet elegant dining room – fitted with idiosyncratic finishings, including a replica Cold War-era missile affixed to the wall – chef Dirk Gieselmann serves up refined and contemporary seasonal German fare with an international twist. It's a set menu, with a particular emphasis on utilising the entire animal, including suckling pig with offal, walnut and onions. Gieselmann's faultless eye for aesthetic detail never detracts from the nuanced flavours, which on any given day might pair pumpkin with watermelon in a hybrid curry with sweet water fish, or local pigeon with cherry compote. Book ahead.

Auguststrasse 11-13

33 00 60 70

S-Bahn Oranienburger
Strasse

Tues–Sat
12pm–4pm, 6–9.30pm
(bar closes 2.30am)

Set menu options
€69–115

W
paulysaal.com

Cordo

The city's favourite wine bar now serving dishes as unique as its wine list.

📍 Grosse Hamburger Strasse 32

📞 27 58 12 15

🚋 S-Bahn Hackescher Markt

🕐 Tues–Sat 6.30pm–12am

€ Set menus €42–105

W cordobar.net

Cordo was never your usual smug wine bar. Founded by four friends in 2013 – two Austrians and two Germans – the theme here was that of cordial rivalry, with the best and most eccentric of both countries represented, served up with brash bites of equally irreverent names like Beets By Dre. In 2018 the team transformed the space into a fully-fledged restaurant, where finely crafted north-German inspired dishes take centre stage alongside the winsome wine list.

Meals come as a set menu – three, five or eight courses: foie gras tacos, veal tongue with roasted leaves or slithers of cod with sweet shallots in a piquant broth. The wine list features some of the Germanic speaking world's chief protagonists, including Wachter-Wiesler, Strohmeier and Weingut Heymann-Lüwenstein – plus minimal intervention wines from the likes of East German export Axel Prüfer, crafting radical wines from France's Languedoc region.

Hotel Adlon

Colloquial street eats at Berlin's most luxurious address.

📍

Unter den Linden 77

📞

22 61 19 59

🚌

S + U-Bahn
Brandenburger Tor

🕐

Mon–Sun 8am–1am

€

€13–25

W

kempinski.com/adlon

Like its city, the Adlon has lived countless lives. Once Europe's most eminent address, the handsome neo-Baroque building adjacent to the Brandenburg Gate (see p.87) has seen some of history's iconic faces stroll through its pirouetting doors: Tsar Nicholas II, Thomas Edison, Albert Einstein, Christopher Isherwood, Charlie Chaplin, Marlene Dietrich and Adolf Hitler. Decimated by World War II, the ruins haunted Pariser Platz for decades.

As the Wall came down, the Adlon rose from the rubble: complete with its centrepiece elephant fountain in the lobby. Whilst well-heeled visitors can enjoy the two Michelin-star Lorenz Adlon Esszimmer, the rest of us can enjoy classic Berliner street food (with a posh twist) in the fabled lobby bar. Don't look past the currywurst, Berliner boulette and the iconic döner kebab with truffled cream, washed down with the famous Elephant Cocktail of gin, rosé, grenadine and grapefruit.

Abends

Katz Orange

*Conscious cooking, with a distinctively
Brandenburg twist.*

Like all good stories the origin of this restaurant begins with a Peruvian
shaman and an orange cat. Legend has it that it was following a visit to said
shaman that Ludwig Cramer-Klett had an epiphany and dreamed up the idea
for this much-loved eatery, named in honour of that very orange cat. Katz
Orange proved a culinary revolution on opening in 2012 – leaping boldly into
the gaping no-man's-land between Berlin's swathe of cheap eats at one end
and its exclusive Michelin-star mavens at the other end – and with a local,
organic and biodynamic focus.

    Set in an atmospheric 19th-century building – a former brewhouse
with distinctive red Prussian brickwork and a splash of Peruvian colour –
this eatery is at once disarming and invigorating, where locally hunted
Brandenburg boar is paired with pickled broccoli, beetroot and walnut and
smoked swedes: ingredients all plenteous in the forests that surround this
otherwise industrial city. While alluring in any season, it's particularly inviting
in summer when you can spill out onto the subtly lit terrace beneath the
ornate brickwork of imperial Berlin – and it's open until 3am.

Bergstrasse 22

Mon–Sun 6pm–3am

€17–30

983 20 84 30

katzorange.com

Tram Pappelplatz

Doyum Restaurant

The lively epicentre of Turkish cuisine in Berlin.

Doyum Restaurant stands tallest amongst the huddle of Turkish eateries in this city. When the West German government originally lured Turkish guest workers north in the 1950s and '60s there was an unanticipated but perfectly delicious side effect – the nation's cuisine got an exciting shot of flavour and flair, manifesting in the most delectable of cultural clashes: the döner kebab, created by Kadir Nurman in 1972. The neighbourhood of Kreuzberg remains the epicentre of Turkish life in Germany, where people gather on benches and in cafes to drink spiced tea, eat baklava and play board games, and families can enjoy the authentic taste of the old country.

Tucked away from the frenetic animation of Kottbusser Tor, Doyum Restaurant is a theatre of scent and colour where a dozen cooks jockey between burners and the laden rotisseries of lamb and beef – and the beguiling aroma of lemon, cumin and sesame accents the air. The Halep is a popular drawcard: succulent lamb carved from the rotisserie and bedded on a rich puree of smoked eggplant, yoghurt and garlic with grilled tomatoes and peppers. Doyum is alcohol-free but has plenty of toothsome Turkish elixirs to choose from and serves up the goodness 'round the clock 24 hours each day.

📍	🕐	€
Admiralstrasse 36	Mon–Sun 24-hours	€5–15

📞	W
61 65 61 27	doyum-restaurant.de

🚍
U-Bahn Kottbusser Tor

Abends

BRLO

Few venues frame the thrilling contemporary zeitgeist of Berlin quite like BRLO.

📍

Schöneberger Strasse 16

📞

55 57 76 06

🚆

U-Bahn Gleisdreieck

🕐

Mon–Sun 12pm–12am

€

€10–25

W

brlo-brwhouse.de

The United States-fuelled craft beer crusade came relatively late to Germany. While other countries were falling head-over heels for hop harried IPAs with staggering alcohol contents, Berliners – and Germans as a whole – watched on with mild bemusement, then strolled back to their local bars to choose a tipple from the country's more than 5000 beer brands.

But Berlin's hugely international population began agitating for the new wave of beer styles – and gypsy brewing outfit BRLO (the Slavic name for Berlin) answered the call with the city's first packaged hop-forward, unpasteurised beers, including a Pale Ale and German IPA. The response was feverish, and BRLO opened its brewery in 2016. It's fashioned from shipping containers, complete with a handsome restaurant and beer garden that – true to maverick form – breaks from tradition, with dishes that cast vegetables in the starring role. The smoked celery with rhubarb, wheat-malt asparagus and German-style kimchi pair perfectly with the smoked beef and dry aged pork belly.

Max und Moritz

Unapologetically 'Old Berlin' with more than a hint of elegance.

📍 Oranienstrasse 162

📞 69 51 59 11

🚆 U-Bahn Moritzplatz

🕐 Mon–Sun 5pm–12am

€ €7–15

W maxundmoritzberlin.de

Max und Moritz carries the mantle of Berliner Küche, celebrating the city's culinary past. It crafts comforting, honest and home-cooked Berliner dishes that are true to region and season, and generally defined by pork, vegetables and sauerkraut.

First opened in 1902, this wirtshaus (tavern) is resplendent with the charms of its epoch: wood panelled and speckled with warm chandelier light. The menu is replete with lost Berliner classics, including Bollenfleisch (lamb stew of winter root vegetables and beer) and the notorious Berliner Eisbein (pickled-then-boiled pork knuckle on a bed of sauerkraut and potato mash). The flammkuchen – otherwise known as tarte flambée – is a favourite with local students, as is the exclusive house beer, supplied by cult breweries Kapuziner and Barre. Max und Moritz takes its name from a cult and darkly humoured German children's story.

Sage Restaurant

*Former rave temple reinvented as a centre
of contemporary haute cuisine.*

They say all punks eventually mellow – and it appears the same is true of
ravers. Berlin's electronic music pedigree is legendary: it stands tall (and
stroboscopic) as the birthplace and spiritual home of techno, along with
Detroit. The Sage Club – alongside the equally fêted Tausend in Mitte –
played a key role in this sonic saga, all from its prime real estate on the
banks of the River Spree. But as Berlin has evolved, so have Tausend and
Sage: now both rehabilitated as discerning culinary hotspots.

Whilst Sage combines Berlin's rustic allure with plush contemporary
trimmings, the menu is a respectful nod to the wider region's culinary history.
Here you'll be served fish sourced from the nearby Baltic Coast, Simmental
beef from Switzerland, Vienna's veal schnitzel and, of course, potato and
cucumber salad: a gratifying fixture of any Berliner kneipe (corner bar-cum-
greasy spoon) worth its salt. But while Sage may have come-of-age, it hasn't
forfeited all of its insurrectionary zeal: now served up as brassy cocktails with
names like Liquid Dancing, It Starts with a Kiss and Between the Sheets,
all crafted to complement the balmy DJ vibes in this premium river setting.

📍	🕐	€
Köpenicker Strasse 18–20	Tues–Sat 6pm–12am	€16–25
📞		W
755 49 40 71		sage-restaurant.de
🚌		
Bus Manteuffelstrasse/Köpenicker Strasse, U-Bahn Schlesisches Tor		

Kanaan

Israeli and Palestinian flavours in central Berlin.

In a city hardly short on falafel and hummus joints, Kanaan perhaps seemed a foolhardy proposition when it first began serving its hybrid Israeli and Palestinian vegetarian cuisine out of a no-frills urban bar in suburban Prenzlauer Berg in 2015. Within months, however, the kitchen had garnered a cult reputation – and partners (both in life and business) Oz Ben David and Jalil Dabit took over a flailing pizza joint directly across the road on Kopenhagener Strasse in Berlin's Scandinavian Quarter: a street fabled for its artist and rustic allure.

Kanaan has never looked back. Hummus is very much the heart of the matter and comes in various delectable guises (Iraqi, Palestinian and Israeli), with the menu featuring falafel, sabach, shakshuka, egg and a heady elixir of spices: best crowned with the house sweet potato fries and a beetroot salad side, accented with goat's cheese and pomegranate, and a glass of the house Syrian wine. Kanaan's success has seen it branch out into Berlin's haughty food temple KaDeWe (see p.59), but its unpretentious digs – perched above the S-Bahn line, just beyond where the Berlin Wall first splintered open on the Bornholmer Bridge on 9 November 1989 – remains its spiritual heartland and a symbol of unity.

Kopenhagener Strasse 17

Tues–Fri 12pm–10pm
Sat–Sun 10am–10pm

€10–20

159 01 34 80 77

kanaan-berlin.de

S + U-Bahn Schönhauser
Allee

Abends

Mrs Robinson's

*An eclectic culinary jewel in Prenzlauer Berg's
charming Helmholtzkiez.*

Samina Raza and Ben Zviel first locked eyes amidst the strobing lights
and throbbing beats of Berlin's notorious Berghain nightclub and would
subsequently go on to forge a partnership in both life and in the larder. The
couple opened Mrs Robinson's: a much-loved haunt that has since developed
from a modest eatery with invigorating Asian influences into one of the city's
most refined – yet unpretentious – contemporary restaurants.

Within its casual New York–style of whitewashed walls, oak
floorboards and wooden benches, chef Ben Zviel's remarkable creations
are the absolute centre of attention. Having worked in kitchens around the
world – including his native Israel and the US – Zviel fuses his passion for
Asiatic flavours (packed with umami) with European ingredients to create
unforgettable plates that both wow and nourish. Every dish on the menu is a
'must-try', but some that you must not bypass are: the Jerusalem artichokes
smothered with a mousse of grapefruit, sunflower seed milk and koji, the
delectably charred octopus and beef skewers and the pike perch parcelled
in roasted leek. Whilst unassuming from the street front, this eatery remains
a Berlin culinary standout, with a menu that's ever-revolving and evolving.

Pappelallee 29   Thurs–Mon 6–10.30pm   €20–40

54 62 28 39   mrsrobinsons.de

Tram Raumerstrasse

Voland

Russian haute cuisine in the heart of old East Berlin.

Voland is an alluring step back into the enchanted Moscow of the poets and thinkers. The Russian spies and apparatchiki may have fled Berlin en masse in 1989 as the first chinks in the Wall began to resound, but the essence of that country – its literature, its songs and its cuisine – never did quite desert East Berlin. As artists and squatters stormed into Prenzlauer Berg to take up residence in the countless abandoned tenements, many locals endured an increasing nostalgia for the old ways: something that came to be known as Ostalgie, or nostalgia for the East.

While much of the Ostalgie of today's Berlin has a level of kitsch about it, Voland is quite the opposite: with sophisticated-yet-comforting dishes, caviar, thimbles of vodka and an ever-pensive troubadour strumming a classical guitar with world-weary paeans to romance and regret. Like the musicians themselves, the food traverses the full breadth of the eastern steppes – from Novosibirsk to Sevastopol, all set in rooms warmly lit by candlelight and chandelier. The weekly music program can be found on the website: book ahead for dinner and show nights.

Wichertstrasse 63

Mon–Sat 6pm–12am

€10–20

444 04 22

voland-cafe.de

S + U-Bahn Schönhauser Allee

Abends

Palsta

Canny Nordic knack in the heart of Neukölln.

Neukölln's transformation has been truly staggering, including the self-proclaimed Nordic Riviera around the Schillerkiez neighbourhood. Once the tired working-class fringe of West Berlin, today the borough has become the centre of Berlin's contemporary dining scene – captained by intrepid international chefs and fuelled by cheap rent. Palsta is one such international fusion: a Danish chef (Filip Søndergaard), a Finnish entrepreneur (Viivi Haussila-Seppo) and perhaps Berlin's finest Scandinavian wine-bar-cum-seafood haunt, where deconstructionist chic meets Baltic pine.

Palsta is Finnish for Schrebergarten – the private garden allotments that can be found all over Berlin. Palsta embodies this very zeitgeist – with stripped-back mottled plaster, exposed bricks throughout and mismatched vases filled with fresh flowers. The cuisine, while equally honest, is also dazzling and the plates are designed to be shared, including seared scallops dressed in salsa, crisp-fried buckwheat with trout roe, and tartare of prawn served on warm rye bread with a pepper speckled mayonnaise and kohlrabi. A variety of natural wines oil this savvy operation. This chic bistro is best enjoyed after a late afternoon stroll in the iconic Tempelhofer Feld (see p.211), across the street.

Oderstrasse 52

176 22 33 06 05

U-Bahn Leinestrasse

Tues 6–11.30pm
Wed–Sat 11am–11pm
Sun 11am–6pm

€5–16

W
palstawinebar.de

Lavanderia Vecchia

Italian cuisine with a fresh Berliner touch.

In a city that has witnessed eateries set up shop in everything from former night clubs to crematoriums, abattoirs and petrol stations, a restaurant in a former laundromat doesn't seem such a stretch of the imagination. Italians play a defining role in this city, and no street is complete without its authentic pizzeria and pasta haunt or Neapolitan-style cafe, spruiking good espresso and heavenly sfogliatella. Lavanderia Vecchia, however, has an altogether different approach – both irreverent in its industrial aesthetic decked out with reclaimed furniture, and wholly serious when it comes to its food. And yes, those are sheets draped all around the restaurant as both a charming installation and a reminder of the room's storied history.

While the kitchen does a discounted pasta lunch offer, the more adventurous set-menu sitting kicks off at 7.30pm, when diners strap in for a journey through the varied regions of Italy. Dishes are brought out at scheduled intervals that last through to around 11pm, with a half bottle of wine per person included in the five-course-set menu price. The service may have a quintessentially Italy-meets-Berlin nonchalance about it, but the nuanced cuisine rarely disappoints. The menu is ever-changing but includes an array of antipasti and gazpacho, followed by two courses – often a risotto variation followed by fish – and dessert. Vegetarian options are available, and a heart-starting coffee is included at the tail-end before you spill out into the midnight air of the city that never sleeps.

Flughafenstrasse 46

Mon–Sat
12pm–3pm & 7.30–11pm

€65

62 72 21 52

lavanderiavecchia.
wordpress.com

U-Bahn Boddinstrasse

Abends

Marjellchen

Memories of Prussia's eastern province on your plate.

📍

Mommsenstrasse 9

📞

88 326 76

🚆

S-Bahn Savignyplatz

🕑

Mon–Sun 5–11.30pm

€

€12–25

W

marjellchen-berlin.de

Berlin's claim to the ultimate seat of German power is rooted in its Prussian heritage. Many Germans from the country's lost eastern provinces (and their ancestors) continue to identify as East Prussian, with a deep nostalgia for its north-eastern landscape, culture and unique cuisine. Marjellchen roughly translates as 'cheeky little girl' in the distinctive East Prussian dialect. It has become the kitchen-table for such memories: a cosy and elegant place.

Here you can enjoy grilled hare in plump cherries, wild boar and deer with cranberries, goulash slow-cooked in layers of onions, marjoram and the revealing accent of caraway (the very essence of East Prussia). Or try the famous Königsberger Klopse: meatballs infused with capers and a hint of Baltic Sea anchovy, served with a beetroot salad – and named for the once grand capital city of this bygone region.

Golden Phoenix

Where Hanoi, Paris, Shanghai and Berlin all intersect.

📍

Provocateur Hotel, Brandenburgische Strasse 21

📞

151 64 62 59 45

🚌

U-Bahn Konstanzer Strasse

🕒

Tues–Sat 6.30–11pm

€

€20–35

W

goldenphoenix.berlin

Chef The Duc Ngo has a progressive attitude to food – elegant yet exhilarating – that has helped transform this city's culinary character. Born in Hanoi to a Vietnamese mother and Chinese father, Golden Phoenix is the nostalgic Chinese dinner table of his past, augmented by the western Europe of his present and future.

Located in the glamourous Provocateur hotel and with velvet chairs and mirrors, this eatery has the opulent atmosphere of a colonial-era French salon. It's a truly sensorial journey: where dim sum take on a new cadence with a hint of truffle, foie gras is dressed with mango and cherry, and the barbary duck brings together two worlds with pumpkin and hoisin. Pair it with the house Weissburgunder (white burgundy, commonly known as pinot blanc), sourced from the Nahe River in the Rhineland.

Abends

Kin Dee

Transformative Thai cuisine with a discernibly 'Berliner' attitude.

The neighbourhood of Schöneberg has always exuded a discernible mix of elegance and moxie – its ornate and elegant 19th-century boulevards and apartment blocks largely left unscathed by the bombs of World War II. But it has also always harboured a subversive edge: a trait that so vibrantly lives on in Kin Dee, one of Berlin's most exciting eateries. Behind its austere facade lies one of the city's most dynamic kitchens: Thai cuisine infused with some serious big-city kudos – a collaboration between Thai-born, New York-raised chef Dalad Kambhu and artist Rirkrit Tiravanija.

Kambhu's imaginative cooking utilises local Germanic ingredients in a Thai context: whole crisp-fried pike perch (a common freshwater fish to most Germans, known locally as zander and usually served with parsley potatoes and swathes of butter) with punchy Thai spices, and parcels of miang kham with crisp endive supplemented for betel leaf. While the dishes explode with fragrance and a kaleidoscope of colour, they strive for simplicity: and are best enjoyed as part of the tasting menu, which comes as either seven, eight or nine courses.

With Berlin awash with pan-Asiatic cuisine, Kin Dee has rattled the local culinary scene to the core and its minimalist furnishings and abstract artworks providing the perfect canvas to enjoy its unique flavours.

Lützowstrasse 81

Tues–Sat 6–10pm

€20–35

215 52 94

kindeeberlin.com

U-Bahn Kurfürstenstrasse

Abends

Fischerhütte am Schlachtensee

Elegant regional fare in a traditional fisherman's lodge set in verdant forest.

If you're lucky enough to visit Berlin in spring you'll be privileged to see a uniquely regional spectacle: the arrival of the much-mythologised white asparagus of Beelitz, a small village south-west of Berlin. And few Berlin-based restaurants pay homage to this prized annual delicacy quite as deliciously as the Fischerhütte – or fisherman's hut – restaurant in Berlin's southern reaches. Beelitz asparagus – or spargel – enjoys protected status in Europe, alongside the prized pecorino of Sardinia, the pinot noir of Burgundy and the Balsamic of Modena. Many Berlin restaurants embrace this tradition, with hand-etched placards announcing the beginning of harvest (usually late April) – albeit to varying degrees of quality. The Fischerhütte is the exception: where this supple and valuable delicacy is afforded reverential treatment, coupled only with hollandaise sauce and new potatoes (you can add rosemary ham or a schnitzel if you desire).

Year-round the Fischerhütte is an elegant stroll back into yesteryear, with comforting dishes all served with an aura of old-world elegance. While the restaurant has a bucolic allure, it is hardly a 'hut' – more a regal country house, perched on the shore of Berlin's most enchanted lake, the Schlachtensee (see p.215). The restaurant also boasts the city's most scenic beer-garden, where simple fare – such as bratwurst, pretzels and roast chicken – is served up with overflowing mugs of pilsner and wheat beer.

The lake is fringed by storybook manor houses, and nearby attractions include Wannsee (see p.213) and Potsdam (see p.105).

Fischerhüttenstrasse 136

Mon–Sun 10am–12am

€10–25

80 49 83 10

fischerhuette-berlin.de

U-Bahn Krumme Lanke

Abends

NACHTS

- night -

It's often said that Berlin belongs to the night. The Berlin Wall fell on 9 November 1989, and the city has been partying hard ever since. Berlin is genuinely a 24-hour city, where it's not uncommon to see all-night revellers sipping G&Ts besides sophisticated brunching crowds at dawn, city workers enjoying a beer with their breakfast and late-risers clasping a cup of coffee at dusk and gearing up for another tilt at the night. Craft beer and natural wine have become permanent fixtures, and Berlin has long had a booming cocktail culture, dating back to its Roaring Twenties when it was notorious the world over for its cabaret clubs, jazz culture and risqué nightlife – so enthrallingly documented by Christopher Isherwood in his Berlin Stories *(see p. 221), later adapted into* Cabaret. *Whether it's the ramshackle chic of Das Hotel (see p. 150) or the very essence of refinement at Ora (see p. 149), Berlin has a bar (and a drink) to satiate all tastes.*

Clärchens Ballhaus

*A true icon of Berlin's nightlife still channelling
the city's golden age of swing and sin.*

The upstairs ballroom at Clärchens Ballhaus wears its vintage with finesse: the walls are gilded with enormous and cracked lead mirrors and the stucco peels from the roof, as though its doors were welded shut following the chaos of war and now only just unsealed to reveal a space where time has stood still. Its 'ruined' interior dating from 1913 – including an ornate panelled balcony and warped chandeliers – tells infinite tales of song, frivolity and wartime fatalism: the room palpable with faded charm and an air of fin de siècle grandeur.

Downstairs the main cavernous ballroom is gilded with tinsel and wood panelling – its dance floor brimming with couples having waltz and foxtrot lessons on any given night, as revellers watch on with glasses of wine and plates of schnitzel. While this downstairs ballroom is open each day, the upstairs ballroom is utilised for special events, including the popular Gypsy Restaurant nights of song, food and much revelry. The beer garden – festooned with tungsten bulbs, trees and the building's rustic brick facade – is ever popular in the warmer months, with crowds spilling out onto Auguststrasse and its coterie of private art galleries.

Auguststrasse 24

282 92 95

S-Bahn Oranienburger
Strasse

Sun–Thurs 11am–12am
Fri–Sat 11am–4am

Deponie Nr. 3

Former tank storage depot reimagined as a unique pub.

Georgenstrasse 4

20 16 57 40

S + U-Bahn Friedrichstrasse

Mon–Fri 9am–1am
Sat–Sun 10am–1am

W
deponie3.de

As unusual Berlin haunts go, this one is a true icon. Housed under the S-Bahn train line in what used to be a military depot for Soviet tank munitions, this atmospheric space offers sanctuary from the summer heat and winter sleet. With a quality range of classic German beer and wines, enjoy a tipple amidst the old-world memorabilia (amongst the throng, are antique advertisements, tools and even a horse carriage) and historic bric-a-brac as the S-Bahn trains rattle overhead.

The bar also features a great menu of Berliner classics, such as kohlroulade (rolled cabbage with pork and gravy), kartoffelsuppe (potato soup) and eisbein (cured and boiled pork knuckle). The apfelstrudel (apple strudel) gives the Austrians a run for their cinnamon.

Café am Neuen See

Picturesque beer garden hemmed by a lake and a towering forest.

📍 Lichtensteinallee 2

📞 254 49 30

🚇 S-Bahn Tiergarten

🕐 Mon–Fri 9am–12am

W cafeamneuensee.de

Set upon the banks of the placid Neuer See lake, this beer garden may be in the very centre of Berlin, but it belongs to another time and place. Enveloped by the leaty Tiergarten park (see p.201) and framed by waterways, there are few more enchanting places to while away an afternoon with a brimming Hefeweizen (wheat beer) and Bretzel (fresh baked pretzel).

German–Jewish Impressionist painter Lesser Ury was particularly fond of this lake and captured its enigmatic charms in the late 19th century. Today you can hire a rowboat and take to its calm waters. As well as unfussy food items at the bar, the cosy onsite restaurant has recently been refurbished.

Luzia

Legendary Kreuzberg venue that dishes out coffee or cava any time of the day.

📍

Oranienstrasse 34

📞

81 79 99 58

🚈

U-Bahn Kottbusser Tor

🕐

Mon–Sun 12pm–5am

W

luzia.tc

When it comes to all things nocturnal, Luzia epitomises Berlin's nightlife. It's a vortex of time and space, where Berliners congregate in the cavernous room, styled with endearing vintage furnishings and always-flattering candlelight, and piece together 'the night before' over cocktails served up by effortlessly hip bar staff. While much of the city's bar scene is consumed with chasing new trends, Luzia forever remains its comforting and welcoming self: a classic Berliner boozery without pretence or pretension, where it's not uncommon to see people popping corks at lunchtime.

Should you feel the need there's also the disco room out back … but most usually settle for a slice of Berliner-style carrot cake stuffed with walnut (a product in plentiful supply in the forests around the city) and a negroni in this beloved Berlin institution. Whether you're here for the beer, beats or bonhomie, Luzia never disappoints.

Prinzipal

Cosy bar that pays tribute to Berlin's swinging 1920s.

📍
Oranienstrasse 178

📞
61 65 45 45

🚇
U-Bahn Kottbusser Tor

🕐
Wed–Thurs 8pm–2am
Fri–Sat 8pm–3am

W
prinzipal-kreuzberg.com

Just when you thought Berlin's bar scene was getting a little too minimal, along comes Prinzipal: a beguiling Kreuzberg bar that takes its cues from the city's golden age of jazz and frivolity. So passionate are this bar's patrons that many frock up in period garb for a night out on the tiles (somewhat literally – and all hand-painted and heritage, may I add). But don't worry if you lack the historic threads as Prinzipal welcomes one and all.

While the space may feel a little intimate, the sights, sounds (including frequent live jazz, cabaret and burlesque), and cocktail list will soon enough free your spirit. The Yin & Yang is a fine curtain-raiser: a footloose olio of Haiti rum, sweet potato, coffee habanero and coconut. Prost!

Yorckschlösschen

*Legendary Kreuzberg jazz bar that's kept Berliners
swinging for over 100 years.*

Artists and jazz musicians have long sought sanctuary in the
Yorckschlösschen: a place to both enjoy a tipple and soak up intoxicating
sounds. When jazz arrived in Berlin in the 1920s, it hit fast and furiously –
the sanguine soundtrack to a new and progressive era of peace and
prosperity under the democratic Weimar Republic (1918–33). War and division
wreaked havoc and ruin, but jazz remained a vital sonorous hallmark of West
Germany – particularly in West Berlin, which was flush with American soldiers
who had access to the latest sounds flooding out of New York and New
Orleans (East Germans on the other side of the Wall were largely incredulous
to the form due to its distinctive American pedigree). Yorckschlösschen
rapidly became the heart of the city's jazz scene.

The dark wood-panelled room is piqued by candlelight and a truly
palpable sense of creative ferment, contrasted by walls decorated with
portraits of a bygone era. While much of the city's nightlife has evolved
beyond all recognition into the 21st century, Yorckschlösschen has
maintained its time-worn allure and dedication to music, including soul and
blues. When there is a live performance, €3–6 is generally added
to patrons' tabs to cover artist fees.

Yorckstrasse 15

Mon–Sat 5pm–3am
Sun 10am–3am

W
yorckschloesschen.de

30 02 15 80 70

Bus Yorckstrasse/
Grossbeerenstrasse

Nachts

Ora

*An elegant haunt that has been dishing out
the medicine since the 19th century.*

Berliners have an uncanny knack for repurposing both time and space.
When in 2015 Lukas Schmid and Christoph Mack took over an old Apotheke
(pharmacy) that had been trading since the mid 19th century, they opted
to preserve the extraordinary trimmings – right down to the atmospheric
wood panelling and medicine cabinets lined with antediluvian jars and
hoary medical paraphernalia of another century. Now complemented by
plush green leather sofas and period furnishings, Ora has since emerged
as one of Kreuzberg's most refined cocktail haunts – with 18 soul-warming
in-house creations.

Whether it be a Chestnut Old Fashioned (rum, chestnut and
angostura) or a Rosemary Manhattan (rosemary, bourbon and rye),
few places dish up such a compelling experience. The wine list is equally
refined – with premium drops from around Europe and a leaning towards
natural wines, including the transcendent Lemberger grape from Roterfaden
Winery in Württemberg: an enigmatic red grape otherwise known as
Blaufränkisch in Austria and Kékfrankos in Hungary, with which German
producers excel.

In recent years Ora has also emerged as a unique dining venue:
serving up small plates composed of ultra-fresh ingredients from surrounding
Brandenburg, including my recommendations: white asparagus served with
pine, pike paired with hazelnut and trout caviar and radish with buckwheat.
There's also a genuine focus on sustainability so you can be sure of the
provenance of your meal.

Oranienplatz 14

54 86 10 70

U-Bahn Moritzplatz

Wed–Sat 6pm–1am
Sun 6pm–12am

W
ora-berlin.de

Das Hotel

*A traditional Berlin
boozery in its hippest hood.*

📍

Mariannenstrasse 26a

📞

84 11 84 33

🚌

U-Bahn Kottbusser Tor

🕐

Mon–Sun 4pm–5am

W

facebook.com/
dashotel.berlin

This classic bar is a portal back into the heady Berlin of the 1990s: a mysterious city full of poise, secrets and promise. It is the epitome of the once-upon-a-time traditional Berlin watering-hole: an evocative all-night bolthole with faded furnishings, peeling stucco, wax-laden candelabras, obscure wall art, a de-tuned piano and ample cheap beer. Thankfully not much has changed at Das Hotel.

But while this place has been fuelling revellers for years it has lost none of its cool; it's a fuss-free zone to relax and sip on bottles of beer and watch the denizens of Berlin stroll (or skate) past, at this bustling intersection between the city's two liveliest boroughs of Kreuzberg and Neukölln. While today a popular pit stop for the international set, it still exudes an unfussy local vibe, with views to the pretty Paul-Lincke-Ufer and canal beyond.

Schankhalle Pfefferberg Braugasthaus

The site of one of the city's oldest breweries refurbished to its former glory.

📍

Schönhauser Allee 176

📞

04 73 77 36 40

🚌

U-Bahn Senefelderplatz

🕐

Tues–Thurs 4pm–12am
Fri–Sat 4pm–1am
Sun 4–11pm

W

schankhalle-pfefferberg.
de/braugasthaus

In the early 19th-century, Bavarian master brewer Joseph Pfeffer moved north to help satiate the thirst of a booming Prussian empire, establishing the Pfefferbräu brewery at this historic site in 1841. It was later sold onto Schneider & Hillig and later again to Berlin brewing behemoth Schultheiss. Decommissioned during the German Democratic Republic (1949–90), the site was refurbished in 2008, with new tenants including a theatre company, Spanish restaurant and this small Schankhalle, or brewpub.

The current brewery embraces the site's historic allure, with handsome copper stills and classic Prussian brickwork – all atop an elevated vantage point over bustling Prenzlauer Berg, with views beyond to the Mitte skyline. Here you'll enjoy beer served fresh from the bright tank. The elegant and tree-lined courtyard is ever-popular in the warmer months.

Nachts

Prater Garten

*The city's original beer garden, flush with history
and house-brewed beer.*

Munich may have the Hofbrauhaus beerhall but Berlin has the Prater Garten. Dating back to 1837, this sprawling beer garden – replete with a country-style log cabin restaurant and historic theatre – has freed the masses from thirst through Prussian conquests, German unification, two world wars and the division and reunification of Berlin. Whilst once on the far-flung fringe of an imperial city, today the Prater Garten sits in the beating chest of Prenzlauer Berg borough and is a convivial meeting place that transcends age, creed and the cut of your breeches.

Many an uprising has been plotted from these hallowed beer benches and today the beer garden maintains its egalitarian zeitgeist: a place where you can enjoy beer, bratwurst and bretzeln (freshly baked pretzels studded with salt) beneath the chestnut trees. Note that the beer garden itself is only open April to September. The bar features two exclusive brews: the pilsner and dunkles (dark beer). And then there's the mythical Berliner Weisse: the slightly sour, low-alcohol wheat beer (galvanised with a shot of saccharine raspberry or woodruff syrup) that once kept this city hydrated – and was immortalised by Viktor De Kowa in song in 1935's *Eine Weisse mit 'nem Himbeerschuss* (*A Weisse with a Raspberry Shot*). The tipple fell from favour in the early 21st century but is now staging a spectacular revival.

The log restaurant is open year-round and is an inspiriting winter escape – with hearty Berliner fare such as duck with red cabbage and roasted goose.

📍
Kastanienallee 7-9

📞
448 56 88

🚇
U-Bahn Eberswalder Strasse

🕗
Beer garden Apr–Sept
Mon–Sun 12pm–12am,
Log restaurant year-round
Mon–Sat from 6pm
until late
Sun from 12pm
until late

W
pratergarten.de

Nachts

Vin Aqua Vin

Take a wine tour of Germany in this welcoming shop-cum-wine-bar.

◉

Schönhauser Allee 176

☎

94 05 28 86

🚋

U-Bahn Hermannplatz

🕑

Mon–Wed 4pm–12am
Thurs–Fri 3pm–12am
Sat 2pm–1am
Sun 4pm–11pm

W

vinaquavin.de

Vin Aqua Vin not only sources its wines directly from the producers, it's also a truly gemütlich (cosy and soul nourishing) space to unwind with a glass under supple candlelight, amidst vintage furnishings and crates of Germany's finest drops.

While many may be able to namecheck a riesling from the fabled terraces of the Rhine River, there is still a great deal of mystery surrounding other German regions and varietals – but the knowledgeable folk at Vin Aqua Vin are here to guide you through. The country officially has 13 major wine regions: amongst the most ethereal being the tiny Ahr Valley (producing truly astounding Spätburgunder, or pinot noir), Württemberg (with its enigmatic red Lemberger grape) and Mosel (with its beguilingly aromatic Weissburgunder, or pinot blanc). All are represented at this welcoming haunt.

Twin Pigs

Embodiment of Neukölln cool with a notorious cocktail menu.

📍
Boddinstrasse 57a

🚇
U-Bahn Rathaus Neukölln

🕑
Mon–Sat 6pm–3am
Sun 6pm–1am

Berlin does austerity like few others. Rough-plastered walls, brindled paint jobs, gritty exposed brick, distressed wood, naked tungsten bulbs and a row of spirit bottles. Welcome to Twin Pigs: your new favourite neighbourhood bar. Created by a Chilean architect and Swedish filmmaker, aesthetic is everything here – from supple candlelight to menus freshly inked on butcher's paper.

The drinks menu is sublime: with crafty cocktails, rare gins and whiskies, sophisticated gin-based longdrinks and a premium beer selection from some of Berlin and Germany's finest boutique brewers. Wines are thoughtfully sourced from mainly organic and biodynamic producers. The bar now features a small-bites menu that promotes ethical nose-to-tail consumption (deep fried lamb's brain included ... with a dash of home-fermented sauerkraut, of course).

Café Rix

A sanctuary of old-world charm tucked away beside a grand old opera house.

_____

📍

Karl-Marx-Strasse 141

📞

686 90 20

🚃

U-Bahn Karl-Marx-Strasse

🕐

Mon–Sun 10am–12am

W

caferix.de

Strolling down the proudly unpolished Karl-Marx-Strasse, with its rows of prefabricated concrete blocks, you certainly don't expect to happen upon Café Rix. It is one of Berlin's most elegant bars, tucked away beside the Neuköllner Oper, one of the city's rare 19th-century opera houses that survived the war and today hosts intimate performances. With timeworn parquet floors, ornamental roof cornicing and supple light, this cafe is a rare window into the alluring Neukölln of centuries passed – when it was known as Rixdorf: a Bohemian quarter fabled for its art, lasciviousness and prodigious boozing.

Today Café Rix is also a rare place to sample Neukölln's beloved kiez brewery, Rollberg: a local outfit that produces fantastic Helles (bright) lager and a red ale, both unfiltered and preservative free. A range of other beverages are also on offer, from coffee to cocktails. It doesn't really matter what you drink, just soak up the surrounds.

Jaja

One of Berlin's leading purveyors of natural wines in Neukölln's thriving Reuterkiez.

📍 Weichselstrasse 7

📞 52 66 69 11

🚌 U-Bahn Rathaus Neukölln

🕐 Tues–Sun 6pm–12am

W jajaberlin.com

Jaja is spearheading Berlin's contemporary wine-bar scene: it's where sophistication meets warm hospitality. It wasn't so long ago when to order a glass of wine in a Berlin bar was a nail-biting gamble that gave little promise beyond a goblet of cheap, cheerless and saccharine Müller-Thurgau (also known as Rivaner) or rough-hewn riesling ... and a sore head. Oh how a decade changes everything.

Whether it be natural or biodynamic, Jaja is a virtual temple to minimal intervention wines from France and beyond, with inviting bottles lining its exposed brick walls. With over 200 wines to explore, including a tongue-twisting line-up of 'orange' wines and pet-nats. Jaja is the ideal haunt to explore the very pointy-end of European viticulture and winemaking. Exquisite plates by chef Yailen Diaz are also on offer – don't look past the smoked eel and sardines in fennel, perfect for sharing on a romantic eve.

Hops & Barley

An urban Berlin-style micro-brewpub where good beer comes before trend.

📍

Wühlischstrasse 22–3

📞

29 36 75 34

🚋

Tram Wühlischstrasse/
Gärtnerstrasse

🕖

Mon–Fri 5pm–1am

Sat 3pm–2am

Sun 3pm–12am

W

hopsandbarley.eu

The ascent of craft beer globally has been swift and spectacular. But Germany has long boasted a vibrant brewing scene: niche and often family owned producers crafting small-batch pilsners, lagers and wheat beers for a loyal following. Hops & Barley is one such haunt: a bolthole suburban Alt Berlin (Old Berlin) style bar, producing some of the finest beers in the city. From its fragrant pilsner to its toothsome red ale and now an American style IPA, there are few more welcoming watering holes.

The petite bar is furnished with a handsome copper still and old Prussian picture tiles from its days as a butcher's shop. The menu includes bite-sized items, such as the Spreewald's legendary gherkins (a true local delicacy, best enjoyed with a slab of rye bread). The bar is ever-popular with locals with an eye for artisan produce, who flock to its outdoor tables in the summer months to enjoy post-work drinks while the sun lingers long into the evening.

Michelberger Café & Bar

One of the city's trendiest addresses, in which to both work and play.

📍

Warschauer Strasse
39–40

📞

29 77 85 90

🚈

S + U-Bahn Warschauer
Strasse

🕐

Mon–Sun 12pm–2am

W

michelbergerhotel.com

The Michelberger Hotel shifted the urban landscape in Berlin and also the once run-down borough of Friedrichshain: now effortlessly hip with a pinch of style and luxury that was once anathema to this part of Friedrichshain. Today the hotel is the go-to destination for rockers and fashion doyens passing through, and its lobby bar has become a beacon for Berlin's transient laptop warriors and after-work revellers, keen to soak up its mash-up aesthetic between playful and austere and enjoy an espresso or Michelberger Sour.

With its sun-laden courtyard, the Michelberger is an urban idyll from where you can while away an afternoon in the company of Berlin's modish denizens. And while you people-watch, you can drink a beer from cult Danish brewery Mikkeller: a pilsner made exclusively for the bar.

Monkey Bar

Chic watering hole with panoramic views over the city.

📍

Budapester Strasse 40

📞

120 22 12 10

🚌

S + U-Bahn Zoologischer Garten

🕐

Mon–Sun 12pm–2am

W

monkeybarberlin.de

As many cyclists would appreciate, Berlin is deadpan flat. While many boroughs in the city wear the suffix 'berg' – or mountain – Berlin is conspicuously devoid of such topographical features, and with it there are very few buildings from whence to get a true bird's (or monkey's) eye view over the city. However, Monkey Bar is one such place: the 10th-floor bar at the 25hours Hotel (part of the Bikini Berlin complex) with a staggering panorama of both the city and the Berlin Zoo below.

But this bar isn't just about the vista – indeed it has become a vibrant emblem of 'New Berlin': bright, brash and bold, with a saga-length cocktail and longdrinks list and chilled sundowner DJ vibes to match the playful interior, of bright furnishings and a much-coveted open-air balcony.

Freischwimmer

Dreamy canal-side escape from the maelstrom of the city.

📍

Vor dem Schlesischen Tor 2

📞

61 07 43 09

🚌

Bus Heckmannufer

🕧

Mon–Thurs 12pm–1am
Fri 12pm–2am
Sat 10am–2am
Sun 10am–1am

W
freischwimmer-berlin.com

While most people dream up abandoned warehouses and industrial scapes when imagining Berlin's bar scene, the city is in fact embroidered with bar and cafe-lined waterways – over 180 kilometres (111 miles) of them, to be exact, drawing comparisons to Venice and Amsterdam. Freischwimmer is one such place: a bucolic wooden shack fringing the Flutgraben canal, which adjoins the River Spree. This area was once a public swimming zone, hence the name, but today is a tranquil urban escape from the clangour of Berlin, where you can enjoy an afternoon waterside beverage and some summer rays.

This historic boat shed also sports an excellent food menu, featuring famous schnitzels, but the most popular takes are the classic German beer and wines on offer to complement the serene surrounds.

JEDERZEIT

– anytime –

This anytime chapter explores many of Berlin's leisure offerings, divided into Märkte (Markets), Einkaufen (Shopping) and Freiluft (Outdoors). Few cities come close to rivalling Berlin's märkte, with its unique array of flea, antique and food markets far-flung across the city. The Mauerpark Flea Market (see p.171) is a magnet for vintage shoppers and the historic indoor Markthalle Neun (see p.167) is the epicentre of the city's kaleidoscopic street food culture. Berlin is also a canny shopper's wonderland, boasting countless boutiques – from vintage through to international luxury labels. The shopping section features nine shopping kieze (neighbourhoods), each promising something truly unique. Many visitors arrive unaware of Berlin's green pedigree. The city has an amazing freiluft (outdoors) culture, bundled with waterways, forested areas, expansive parklands and lakes, which make for enchanting day trips. Must-dos include the serene Wannsee lake (see p.213) and the tranquil central park, the Tiergarten (see p.201).

Zeughaus Art Market

*Unique original artworks for sale and a good starting
point to get a taste of the city's creative drive.*

Berlin Is one of the world's truly inspired cities: a pilgrimage for both artists and art lovers keen to explore beyond the frontiers of their imaginations. While the city remains synonymous with street art, many practitioners – both traditional and those at the coalface of new and experimental artistic forms – convene at the Zeughaus Art Market to spruik their wares. It is a great place to gauge the city's artistic pulse before digging deeper into its endless catalogue of public and private galleries.

The market boasts dozens of stalls lining the River Spree – in the shadows of Unter den Linden's oldest building, now the Deutsches Historisches Museum (German Historical Museum, see p.85) – featuring artists, artisans and designers, selling everything from original paintings and carvings to handcrafted jewellery.

A visit to this weekend market is well paired with the Antique and Book Market, which takes place 500 metres (1640 feet) north along the river, in front of the imposing Bode Museum, where you'll find stunning examples of genuine antique jewellery, collectible tomes and historic artworks offloaded by family estates. While some stallholders accept credit card, cash is advised. Opening times below are applicable to both markets.

Am Zeughaus 1–2

Sat–Sun 11am–5pm

S-Bahn Hackescher Markt

Markthalle Neun

*Historic indoor market that has undergone
a hip-replacement.*

By the 1990s, Berlin's 19th-century market halls were all but extinct –
a victim of German's ultra-competitive supermarket landscape. Of the
original 14 traditional indoor market halls, only three have survived in their
official form, and Markthalle number IX (Neun) in Kreuzberg was perilously
close to its date with the demolition ball. Skip forward to 2011 and – thanks
to the guerrilla actions of local residents – the gates of the market hall swung
open once more, albeit with a discernibly contemporary nip and tuck.

Markthalle Neun has become the symbolic nerve centre of Berlin's
food revolution: a champion of organic (locally known as bio) products and
a pioneer of the city's international street food movement, with Street Food
Thursday perennially one of Berlin's most vibrant culinary and social events.
The lofty hall remains an inspired place to purchase artisan smallgoods,
wine, vegetables and baked goods for picnics, with plenty of international
street food vendors to entice you to stay just a little longer ... abetted by the
Heidenpeters craft beer corner, where beer is brewed directly on site.

Eisenbahnstrasse 42–3

U-Bahn Görlitzer
Bahnhof

Mon–Wed & Fri
12pm–6pm
Thurs 12pm–10pm
Sat 10am–6pm

Kollwitzplatz Farmers' Markets

*The city's most picturesque markets with food
and artisan wares.*

Long before Berlin underwent its 21st-century culinary revolution, the Saturday Kollwitzplatz Farmers' Markets were a bastion of rare produce, impeccable taste and much bonhomie. It was – and still is – a culinary sanctuary that offers local delicacies, such as white asparagus, wild pfifferlinge (chanterelle mushrooms), Feldsalat (Rapunzel lettuce) and incandescent raspberries, all harvested from nearby fields in Brandenburg that very morning. Bag some organic wildschwein loin (wild boar), a slab of rustic landbrot (farmer's loaf, often using rye and spelt) and toast your loot with a glass of Grauburgunder (pinot gris) and a plate of oysters on your way out. Little has changed from its exhilarating founding days: a few more stands spruiking children's clothing and tourist trinkets (and a great deal more visitors), but otherwise this beguiling market has remained just that.

The Saturday market is complemented by an organic food market on Thursdays, which has promoted good farming practice and consumer knowledge for well over two decades; ambrosial local honeys, crates of Brandenburg's famed apples, preserves crafted from indigenous elderberries and even detoxifying birch sap have been harvested from the many biospheres surrounding Berlin. Alternatively, you can opt for the ancient German elixir of birch sap wine.

Kollwitzplatz is a favourite destination for families, as the square is well-equipped with playgrounds – all in the purview of a statue of Käthe Kollwitz: the artist and former resident for whom the square, street and kiez (neighbourhood) are named.

Kollwitzstrasse 64–8

U-Bahn Senefelderplatz

Farmers' Market
Sat 9.30am–4.30pm
Organic Food Market
Thurs 12pm–7pm

Mauerpark Flea Market

Once a wasteland between East and West,
now an iconic market.

Looking for that rare East German punk record or a desk chair from Imperial Prussia? Or maybe a perfectly worn chandelier or a dog-eared painting of a Berlin streetscape that was lost to bombs and history? Well, this iconic park is your place. The borough of Prenzlauer Berg played a pivotal role in the Wende (peaceful revolution) that swept across East Germany in 1989. When the Wall finally fell it was here, at the Bornholmer Strasse border crossing into the Allied borough of Wedding – also known as the Bösebrücke (Bornholmer Bridge Crossing) – when at 11.30pm on 9 November 1989, after a shaky start, thousands of people began streaming into West Berlin. Mauerpark – or Wall Park – soon after became a place of convergence, contemplation and annual May Day mayhem.

Today the otherwise austere park is celebrated as a parapet of free expression – where people from the world-over come to busk, breathe fire, graffiti paint, tightrope and people watch: namely on Sundays, when 'Bearpit Karaoke' takes over the stone amphitheatre (one microphone, thousands of baying spectators) and the fabled flea market opens its doors. Once a place to pursue seemingly infinite rows of 19th-century chandeliers, antique paintings and rare Schlager records (a curious form of German turbo-folk-pop that only makes sense with ample schnapps), today the park is brimming with artisans, curiosities, street food and – of course – retro threads. Mauerpark remains a genuine Berlin institution.

9
Bernauer Strasse 63–4

🕑
Sun 10am–6pm

W
flohmarktimmauerpark.de

🚋
Tram Friedrich-Ludwig-
Jahn-Sportpark,
U-Bahn Eberswalder
Strasse

Maybachufer Turkish Market

*A kaleidoscopic selection of Turkish products
to electrify the senses.*

Today people of Turkish origin represent around five percent of Germany's population, and more than seven percent in Berlin, which boasts the largest Turkish population outside Turkey. Each Tuesday and Friday the picturesque Maybachufer along the Landwehr Canal becomes a prismatic display of Turkish sights and senses: tomatoes, blood oranges, lemons and pomegranates all sun-kissed by the Aegean and Mediterranean sun, golden baklava speckled with crushed pistachios, freshly prepared gözleme generously laden with spinach and goat's cheese, and a vivid display of herbs, spices and smallgoods. Tattooed Berlin punks, enthralled tourists and women in traditional headscarves all jostle for space amidst the laden stalls, where you'll find all your essentials including leopard-print fabric and an extravagant array of slinky underwear.

To paint the backstory of Turkish immigration to Germany, by the 1950s the West German Wirtschaftswunder (economic miracle) had seen the country's economy thrive once again. However, having sacrificed well over four million of its young men in the war, West Germany turned to Turkey, and the Gastarbeiter (guest worker program) was initiated. Over the decades the Turkish community has become a vital component of Berlin's identity and also brought much-savoured spice and flare to the local culinary landscape, best experienced at these unique markets.

Maybachufer   Tues & Fri 11am–6.30pm

U-Bahn Schönleinstrasse

Grosser Antikmarkt am Ostbahnhof

Nostalgic antique market crammed with
East German rarities.

Ostalgie – or the nostalgia for East Germany – comes in many forms. For some it is the memory of a guaranteed job and salary, for others, it's the simple joys of free body culture (nude bathing and perhaps a spot of nude volleyball) with three generations of your family at the Baltic Sea. For others still, it's a colossal Spreewald pickles and Vita Cola: East Germany's viscous answer to Coca Cola (with its own closely guarded recipe). Whatever your East German craving, you're quite likely to find it at the antique market behind the busy Ostbahnhof train station.

A traditionally working-class area still largely untouched by the sheen of gentrification, this eclectic market offers a rare and often intimate insight into life through the purview of an East German lens: from German Democratic Republic (GDR) military medallions to personal photo albums; from bygone Ostmark (the GDR's currency) to Soviet folk LPs; from postcards to GDR cookbooks, featuring recipes for such enduring East German classics as jägerschnitzel: 'hunter's schnitzel' spiced with Soviet (Hungarian) paprika, and usually complemented by seasonal mushrooms. Garnished with a healthy dose of kitsch, this market is an endearing stroll through a country that time is in danger of forgetting.

Erich-Steinfurth-Strasse 1

Sun 9am–5pm

S-Bahn Ostbahnhof

Boxhagener Platz Flea Market

*Bric-a-brac Sunday market and retro miscellany
that never fails to dazzle.*

Ever fancied taking a poised self-portrait with a long-forgotten brand of 1970s Japanese camera through the reflection of a splintered 19th-century lead mirror wearing a replica Soviet gas mask? Well at the Boxhagener Platz flea market you can finally tick this wish off ... and so, so much more. This iconic market boasts everything you ever wanted – that you never knew you wanted. A burnished candelabra in the form of an octopus? Done! A bust of Winston Churchill that doubles as an ash tray? Sorted! An East German Telefunken television that only transmits long-extinct station frequencies from the days of the GDR? Yes please!

This market takes place every Sunday in Friedrichshain's most handsome square and is a veritable feast of possibilities – and not all so miscellaneous. Those with a discerning eye swear by the potential to nab an historic heirloom, a finely crafted instrument or genuinely rare vintage garment. The bustling atmosphere is most often soundtracked by a medley of international buskers. A stand serves classics such as currywurst: an historic symbol of 'Allied' culinary diplomacy, reputedly created by grill Svengali Herta Heuwer in West Berlin shortly after World War II: a holy trinity of ketchup (US), curry powder (UK) and bratwurst (Germany). The French – the other Allied force in West Berlin – politely abstained from contributing to the recipe.

◉
Boxhagener Platz 1

◷
Sun 10am–6pm

🚌
Bus Boxhagener Platz,
Tram Wühlischstrasse/
Gärtnerstrasse

Arminiusmarkthalle

*A 19th-century market where tradition
trumps trends.*

Honest Berlin traders line the cavernous interior of this market to sell their wares: from fishmonger and antique book trader, wine merchant and baker, to grocer and sausage maker. Indeed, Berlin often feels so international and modish it begs the question: where have all the real Berliners gone? The answer is: here, to the Arminiusmarkthalle. Traditional haunts such as Arminiusmarkthalle are mournfully of a dying breed. Like the traditional kneipe (corner pub) these time-worn heirlooms are rapidly disappearing as Berlin sprints into the 21st century.

Despite its central location, Moabit has maintained its moxie in the unrelenting flurry of gentrification, manifested in this central market hall which, while splendidly reappointed in all its 19th-century glory, is where people come to shop ... not masquerade.

Unfussy jars of enormous Spreewald pickles line the counters where stallholders do a brisk trade, and the crates of just-picked Brandenburg apples line the hallways ready to be snapped up. And when you're done shopping, you should eat like a local: with a plate of pickled herring from the Baltic Sea, a Schrippe (rustic white bread roll) and a bottle of unfussy Berliner Pilsner. Prost!

Arminiusstrasse 2–4

Mon–Sat 9am–10pm

arminiusmarkthalle.com

U-Bahn Turmstrasse

Weihnachtsmärkte
(Christmas Markets)

*In late November through December Berlin softens
its edge to become a Yuletide wonderland.*

If you are lucky enough to visit Berlin in December you won't want to avoid
this fabled festive phenomenon. For all the city's radical zeal, when it comes
to Christmas Berliners are sticklers for tradition. And tradition dictates that
demountable wooden huts be interspersed around the city to delve up ladles
of glühwein (mulled wine), candied almonds, Stollen (fruitcake), Lebkuchen
(gingerbread) and steaming plates of Käsespätzle (egg noodles pan-fried in
butter and laden with melted cheese, and usually served up with ham and
crisp fried onion). You can't help but get caught up in the Christmas cheer –
as families and friends gather to enjoy a steaming cup beneath the supple
Christmas lights and watch the snowflakes fall. Look out for the garish 'mega
winter compounds' that sprout up at Alexanderplatz (see p.81), Unter den
Linden (see p.85) and Potsdamer Platz (see p.91), complete with corn dogs and
fairground fixtures – although note that many Berliners prefer to dodge these.

For the quintessentially 'traditional' Berlin Weihnachtsmarkt experience,
head to Gendarmenmarkt (see p.89): the city's most enchanting and
atmospheric market (entry €1, which goes to charity), where you'll find a heady
assortment of foods, artisanal producers, handcrafts and, of course, soothing
Glühwein (with or without a cheeky dash of Amaretto). The following traditional
Christmas markets are also all well worth a visit: Spandau, Domäne Dahlem,
Alt-Rixdorf, Schloss Charlottenburg and Lucia Markets at the village-like
KulturBrauerei in Prenzlauer Berg. For those craving a discernibly more 'cool
Berlin' fix, the hip Christmas market Holy Shit Shopping (holyshitshopping.de)
is a perennial favourite, with fashion, food and ironic Christmas trinkets.

📍

Various locations

🚋

U-Bahn Stadtmitte

🕑

December

2–8pm

(individual market

hours vary)

W

visitberlin.de/en/
christmas-markets-berlin

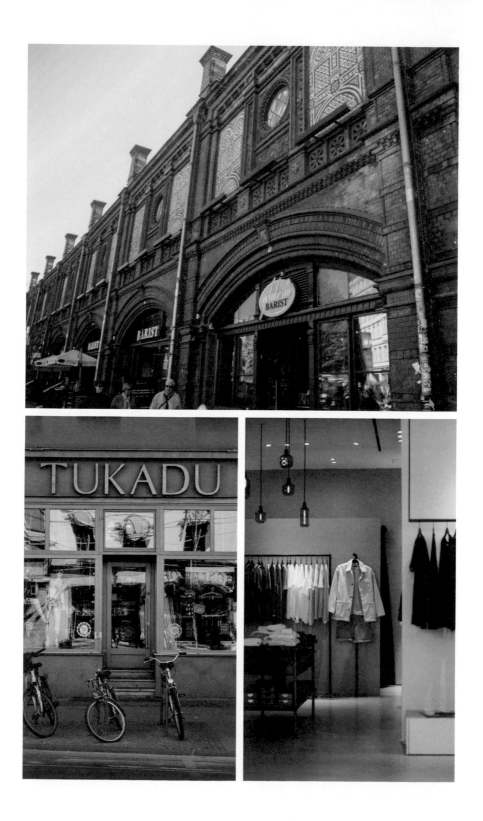

Hackescher Markt

*The centre of reunified Berlin: where history
and the hip-pocket meet.*

Historically, East Berlin had Alexanderplatz (see p.81) and West Berlin
had Charlottenburg – and now reunified Berlin has Hackescher Markt: the
symbolic shopping centrum of these two old foes. The entry point to Museum
Island (see p.69), Hackescher Markt sits just north of the river between
Rosenthaler Strasse and Neue Schönhauser Strasse (plus west both along
Oranienburger Strasse and Sophienstrasse). It has emerged as a thriving
commercial borough – famed for its flagship brand outlets, such as Nike and
Puma ... the latter created by German Rudolf Dassler, brother (and bitter
rival) to Adolf Dassler, the founder of adidas. As well as numerous fashion
boutiques by the likes of Ben Sherman, Hugo Boss and Brandy Melville,
the borough is notable for its boggling number of shoe stores, amongst
them a flagship store for German's totemic footwear brand, Birkenstock.
Oranienburger Strasse get a little more edgy with its fashion offerings, but
often still comes with a hefty price-tag.

Beyond its shopping drawcards, the Hackescher Markt square outside
the resplendent train station of the same name – admired for its Prussian
brickwork – is home to a small artisan market each Thursday and Saturday
during daylight hours, selling everything from homemade wooden sunglasses
to pottery and second-hand clothing. While small, this square has emerged as
the city's unassuming centre where many large chain restaurants and coffee
shops spill out onto the cobbled terrace and trams rattle past and onward to
the city's eastern reaches (only East Berlin maintained its historic tramlines,
with the West opting for the somewhat less romantic bus).

📍

Hackescher Markt,
between Rosenthaler &
Neue Schönhauser strasse

🚌

S-Bahn Hackescher Markt

🕗

Mon–Sat
10am–6pm
(individual store
hours vary)

Torstrasse

*This periphery road between Mitte and
Prenzlauer Berg has had a designer makeover.*

Just 20 years ago Torstrasse was, to borrow from the colourful 'Berliner Schnauze' (Berliner snout) lexicon, a Drecksloch (to put it politely … a dirt hole). Little more than a blustery East Berlin tramway sporting dilapidated buildings and blistering asphalt, few could have predicted its swift resurrection. Today the street has not only been rejuvenated, it has been completely reborn as a boulevard of boutique hotels, urbane bars, a genuinely thrilling dining scene and – naturally – designer shops, albeit still with a discernibly Berlin vibe.

Searching out that casual pair of retro €350 sunglasses? This is your place (try Lunettes). A one-of-a-kind pair of adidas sneakers inspired by the upholstery in Berlin's underground trains, with an annual train travel pass sewn into the tongue? Well, you're in luck (Kickz awaits)! Whether you plan to pop into Soho House (Berlin's first 'exclusive membership' haunt for the upwardly mobile) for a spa-side cocktail, or seek out an oatmilk flat white-style coffee with the perfect micro-foam at one of the countless cafes lining the strip (Röststätte on the corner of Ackerstrasse always dazzles), Torstrasse won't fail you.

For those needing to atone their capitalistic sins at the day's end, the nearby Volksbühne theatre is the home of Berlin's most radical theatre troupe, tracing its ideological ancestry to East Berlin, with its enduring motto: 'Die Kunst dem Volke' (the art belongs to the people).

Torstrasse

U-Bahn Rosenthaler Platz

Mon–Sat
10am–6pm
(individual store
hours vary)

Friedrichstrasse

*Inner-city shopping on one of Berlin's
most sophisticated streets.*

The central borough of Mitte's rehabilitation has been staggering. Only
two decades ago this was one of the largest building sites on earth, still
blighted by the wounds of war, as East Germany had turned its attention
towards Alexanderplatz (see p.81) to be its new architectural and commercial
showpiece. Formal reunification in 1990 placed Mitte firmly back in the, well,
'middle' of Berlin (being the very meaning of the word), and painstaking
restoration work began. Friedrichstrasse has since emerged as a symbol
of unity: its facades restored, gaping holes reimagined with sympathetic
architecture and most of it dedicated to central European fashion.

Jewellery and fashion brands, such as Swarovski, Karl Lagerfeld,
Hugo Boss and Massimo Dutti, have stores here. The northern end – towards
Friedrichstrasse train station – however, becomes noticeably less ritzy, with
cut-price shoe outlets and sporting-wear. Here you can lose yourself in the
much-treasured Berlin institution Dussmann: a five-level temple dedicated to
books, including a well-stocked international section. The store also features
an impressive music division – including shelves laden with vinyl – and is
fabled by collectors for its extensive comic selection. When you're done stroll
down to Deponie Nr. 3 (see p.142) for a refreshing post-retail ale.

Friedrichstrasse 1

S + U-Bahn
Friedrichstrasse

Mon–Sat
10am–6pm
(individual store
hours vary)

Bergmannkiez

*Picturesque locale with a fine assortment
of upmarket boutiques.*

While much of inner-city Berlin has been preoccupied with rapid
transformation, Bergmannkiez has busied itself with quite the contrary:
staying its charming old self. Very few quarters exude the grace of this
highly coveted area of Kreuzberg: its undulating cobbled lanes and perfectly
restored apartments often feeling more Parisian than Prussian. Buttressed
by the peaceful Kirchhof Luisenstadt cemetery at one end and the lush
Viktoriapark at the other, the streets between are inhabited with a range
of clothing boutiques, speciality wine stores and special interest shops –
including a juggling supplies store, if you plan to busk on your travels.

The streets south of the Gneisenaustrasse U-Bahn train station
are a true pleasure to lazily meander, with plenty of unique eateries to
refuel at. The Marheineke Markthalle remains one of Berlin's last remaining
19th-century market halls and has a range of artisan stalls, eateries and
a supermarket. Living up to its liberal leanings, the nearby Passionskirche
(Passion Church) has become a stunning and truly unique venue for
international music concerts, complete with a well-stocked bar to satiate
the communion. The program is available on the website (akanthus.de), and
tickets usually sell out in advance.

Marheinekplatz 1

U-Bahn Gneisenaustrasse

Mon–Sat
10am–6pm
(individual store
hours vary)

Kastanienallee

*Eclectic boutique brouhaha in the heartland
of old East Berlin.*

In the years following reunification, all eyes turned to Prenzlauer Berg: a
gritty working-class borough that architecturally had largely survived World
War II and became a haven for subversive communes and experimental
artists. Whilst today the once-monochrome buildings have been given a
fresh lick of plaster and paint, and the occupied squats have all but been
ceded to developers, Kastanienallee – or the Avenue of Chestnuts, a main
thoroughfare linking Prenzlauer Berg and Mitte – maintains its eclectic
vibe of small boutiques, shopfronts selling handmade wares, gift shops and
record stores.

     The crossroad section with Oderberger Strasse is particularly popular –
the aforementioned street famous for its vintage clothing stores, which are
the curtain-raiser to the Saturday flea markets in the Mauerpark (see p.171)
at the end of the street. Kastanienallee is also home to one of Berlin's more
iconic urban cinemas, Lichtblick-Kino, which usually screens subversive
and political films. Next door, the Tuntenhaus squat at Kastanienallee 86
maintains the rage, with its now iconic slogan written on the building's
facade: 'Capitalism normalises, kills, destroys.' Whether you agree or not,
you'll be made to feel welcome, and the house often spruiks original artworks
and handcrafts. And no day of shopping is complete without a welcome drink
at the Prater Garten (see p.153), Berlin's most historic beer garden.

Kastanienallee

U-Bahn Eberswalder
Strasse

Mon–Sat
10am–6pm
(individual store
hours vary)

Schillerkiez

*A most dapper quarter of Neukölln with an eclectic
blend of shops and emporiums.*

While the borough of Neukölln's rise as the headquarters of Berlin's
international hipster set has been relatively swift, Schillerkiez – one of
Neukolln's many unique kieze (neighbourhoods) – has long had a hint of
suave about it. With its well-preserved apartment blocks, cobbled streets
and front-row vistas onto both the Tempelhofer Feld park (see p.211), and
beautiful Hasenheide park (see p.205), it exudes a rustic tranquillity and
casual elegance that sets it apart from its neighbouring kiez. Neukölln's
contemporary (and highly international) food movement began right here in
Schillerkiez – what's often only half-joking called the Nordic Riviera due to its
large number of Scandinavian expats – and similarly the area has seen the
rise of numerous shopfronts and boutiques emerging from its gridded streets
north of Leinestrasse U-Bahn train station.

The kiez centres around the Herrfurthplatz – a quaint circular plaza,
which is home to the Schillermarkt: a small market with a restaurant and
cafe. Stretching out from here you'll find bolthole stores selling everything
from natural wine to 'retro' 1990s curiosities; and vegan gift boutiques to
high-end vintage shops. Be sure to check out both Treasures of the '90s
(clothing) and Süssstoff (gifts and curiosities). Artisans and hawkers often sell
their wares at the entrance to Tempelhofer Feld on Herrfurthstrasse on the
weekends. When you're done scouring the many pop up shops and boutiques
then retire to Palsta (see p.129) for some fine Nordic fare.

Herrfurthplatz

U-Bahn Leinestrasse

Mon–Sat
10am–6pm
(individual store
hours vary)

Boxhagener Kiez

*East Germany's grungy frontier with truly
unique offerings.*

Today the Boxhagener kiez (neighbourhood) has emerged as one of the
city's more interesting quarters: a stirring area of working-class locals,
international creatives and young families. Large swathes of the borough still
proudly wear their grey and crumbled facades as a badge of anti-capitalist
distinction, which has attracted a creative community – lured by the idea of
self-determined individuality. But now there's small boutiques selling unique
wares, handcrafts and designer children's clothing.

While the flea market at Boxhagener Platz (see p.177) – a short walk
north of Warschauer Strasse S and U-Bahn train stations – has achieved
folklore, the surrounding streets are well worth a visit in their own right, lined
with boutiques of every shade. Kopernikusstrasse and Grünberger Strasse –
and the tributary streets between – offer the best array: from homemade
jewellery and tattoo parlours, to vintage-inspired clothing and antique book
peddlers. If it's in your wildest dream, you'll likely find it here. When you've
bagged your loot head to the local favourite Hops & Bailey (see p.158) for
a house-made brew of the highest order.

Kopernikusstrasse &
Grünberger Strasse

Bus Boxhagener Platz,
Tram Wühlischstrasse/
Gärtnerstrasse

Mon–Sat
10am–6pm
(individual store
hours vary)

Kurfürstendamm

*Old Berlin's most luxurious shopping destination
rebooted for the 21st century.*

This fabled strip takes its name from the Kurfürsten, who were the prince
electors of Brandenburg: representatives of the Holy Roman Empire that
once ruled over these lands. As its name suggests, this commercial artery
maintains its regal touch – once the showpiece of West German decadence
and today an intoxicating area of old-world charm, splendid boutiques and
a newfangled contemporary edge.

The main section of shopping is contained in the 800-metre (2624
feet) stretch between the U-Bahn train stations Wittenbergplatz and
Kurfürstendamm, where Tauentzienstrasse becomes Kurfürstendamm. Here
you'll find that historic temple to opulence, the KaDeWe (see p.59), with its
floors of haute couture and traditional designer brands – and, of course, its
famous delicatessen where it'd be remiss not to stop to rest your feet over
oysters and champagne. Behind the Kaiser Wilhelm Memorial Church (see
p.97) stands one of the city's most chichi shopping addresses: Bikini Berlin,
on Budapester Strasse. Part pop-up palace, part Instagrammer fairyland, this
multi-storey shrine to bespoke fashion is certain to throttle your unassuming
credit card.

Kurfürstendamm

Mon–Sat
10am–6pm
(individual store

U-Bahn Kurfürstendamm

hours vary)

Schlossstrasse

*Upper-middle class borough lined with department
stores and speciality shops.*

While Steglitz may lack some of the heavy-hitting tourist sites and urban
street credibility, it's nonetheless an elegant borough of well-groomed 19th-
century manors and cobbled backstreets – and was once the second largest
shopping precinct in West Berlin. Little has changed since then: the area has
retained its distinctive charm and continues to be an increasingly popular
destination for shopping, largely thanks to its well-appointed department
stores and varied fashion outlets. Schlossstrasse exudes an air of refinement
and makes for a satisfactory day of shopping and exploration, all within easy
strolling distance of the Rathaus Steglitz S and U-Bahn train stations.

 The area is largely known for its large outlets and department stores –
including a giddying array of shoe shops, as well as mid-tier fashion outlets
and jewellery emporiums – and is a veritable one-stop street for shoppers in
Berlin's well-heeled southern reaches. Das Schloss – The Palace – is the most
exemplary department store on Schlossstrasse: with over 80 shopfronts for
which Berliners and tourists travel from miles around, situated just across
from the borough's most iconic landmark, the 19th-century redbrick Rathaus
(town hall). When you've had your shopping fix, jump back on the S-Bahn
train line and head a few stops south to one of the city's most coveted
eateries: the Fischerhütte am Schlachtensee (see p.137), perched at the
banks of the city's most alluring lake (the Schlachtensee, see p.215) and with
a welcoming beer garden.

Schlossstrasse 37

S + U-Bahn Rathaus
Steglitz

Mon–Sat
10am–6pm
(individual store
hours vary)

Tiergarten

Berlin's central park is speckled with lush gardens, lakes, brooks and grass meadows.

The Tiergarten is a 210-hectare (518-acre) oasis in the middle of the bustling city. Once a royal hunting ground flush with boar and deer and connected to the City Palace by a bridle trail (now Unter den Linden, see p.85), today the Tiergarten belongs to the people. It's buttressed at its southern end by Berlin Zoo: the most visited zoo in Europe, and with over 20,000 animals (most famous being its lions and hippos) is well worth a half day – especially if you're travelling with children. Stippled with winding pathways and waterways, it's easy to get lost in the Tiergarten and difficult to imagine you're in the middle of an otherwise lively city. But even if you're lost, fear not: the park is safe and frequent signs map out the park's many pathways and exit points. And if you can't find any signs, you're bound to happen upon picnickers, sunbathers or joggers who can help point the way.

The park is speckled with statues and monuments dedicated to the Hohenzollern dynasty, and at the centre is the towering Siegessäule (Victory Column), marking 19th-century Prussian victories, atop which an icon of Victoria strides in triumph: locals endearingly call her 'Goldelse' (Golden Lizzy). The park is also home to two tempting beer gardens: Cafe am Neuen See (see p.143) and the Schleusenkrug at the western fringe; a statue to controversial German composer Richard Wagner; and a Soviet war monument (replete with tanks). There's a memorial to socialist revolutionary Rosa Luxemburg, whose murder followed the Spartacist Uprising of 1919, when her body was dumped in the park's Landwehr Canal. Separate monuments to the homosexual and Sinti and Roma victims of National Socialism can be found at the eastern end of the park.

Tiergarten

S + U-Bahn
Brandenburger Tor,
S-Bahn Tiergarten

Volkspark Humboldthain

Tranquil park named for the natural historian
Alexander von Humboldt.

The Humboldthain park offers a slice of tranquillity in the heart of the city and has some of the city's highest peaks and undulating walking trails, for those seeking an hour or three of respite. The Humboldt brothers left an indelible mark on their home city. While Wilhelm made his name as a philosopher and diplomat, Alexander is best remembered as a naturalist, geographer and intrepid explorer and the first person to document the phenomenon of human-engendered climate change in 1800. The Humboldthain People's Park is named in honour of Alexander.

With scenic walkways and chromatic gardens, including the rose garden with ornate hedgerows, the Humboldthain also features one of Berlin's last remaining anti-aircraft flak towers, which is easy to climb, with free entry and offers a vast panorama of Berlin's northern reaches and into Brandenburg beyond (a rare vista for most visitors, as most tourist sites are situated in the city's centre and southern reaches). If travelling with children, the park also features a public swimming pool and popular water playgrounds with waterslides – a perfect summer escape, and one extremely popular with the locals.

The Humboldthain is also home to a small vineyard that produces modest amounts of riesling, albeit not yet for sale, due to Europe's strict appellation laws, which currently do not recognise Berlin as a wine-producing region: something likely to change as, so astutely observed by Alexander Humboldt, the region increasingly experiences warmer temperatures.

Volkspark Humboldthain

S + U-Bahn Berlin-
Gesundbrunnen

Hasenheide

*Historic park with a monument
to Berlin's 'rubble women'.*

This splendid park, which translates to Rabbit Warren and was a former regal hunting ground, sits between the boroughs of Kreuzberg and Neukölln and dates from 1678. However, its more recent history is what now defines it: with Berlin in ruins following World War II and most of its young men dead, wounded or imprisoned, the monumental clean-up job was largely left to the city's women. The Trümmerfrau (rubble women) have become icons of Berlin's onerous recompense and renewal – and today a sculpture in the Hasenheide park and gardens marks their colossal efforts. You'll find it at the foot of the Rixdorfer Höhe: a 68-metre (223 feet) hill constructed from 700,000 cubic metres of war rubble.

Situated between two of the city's most lively boroughs, the park is a magnet for sun-seekers and strollers, with vast open meadows to kick a ball or laze with a book, forested areas with ambling pathways and even a small mini-golf course and children's animal farm. In summer the park is home to one of the city's most picturesque freiluftkinos (outdoor cinemas). The park is considered the birthplace of Germany's gymnastics movement (founded by Friedrich Ludwig Jahn in 1811) and is the site of the famous duel in Theodor Fontane's 1895 realist novel *Effi Briest*: the *Anna Karenina* of German literature.

Hasenheide

U-Bahn Hermannplatz

Volkspark Friedrichshain

*Berlin's oldest public park with a monument
celebrating German fairy tales.*

Famed for an enchanting fairy tale fountain, this remains one of the city's finest parks – rolling open spaces surrounded by trees and winding paths, with splendid fountains, a Japanese pavilion and an amphitheatre, which in summer hosts one of the city's most popular freiluftkinos; or outdoor cinemas. The Märchenbrunnen (Fountain of Fairy Tales) at the entrance of Friedrichshain's 'People's Park' – is a Neo-Baroque tribute to the ever-intoxicating fairy tales collected by the Brothers Grimm, amongst them *Cinderella, Little Red Riding Hood, Snow White and the Seven Dwarfs* and *Sleeping Beauty*. In 1840 Jacob and Wilhelm Grimm travelled to Berlin, at the invitation of Friedrich Wilhelm IV, to take up positions at the University of Berlin, now Humboldt University. The fountain was designed by architect Ludwig Hoffmann and completed in 1913.

In the park, you'll also see the Peace Bell in the Japanese gardens – a gift from Japan to East Berlin in 1989 as a unified symbol against nuclear warfare. Or join the locals and unwind at the historic kiosk, with an Alster (a pilsner mixed with lemonade) or Bionade (a favourite herbal soft drink). At the centre of the park is a small yet charming lake – an ideal spot to relax and take in the natural beauty. The historic green space also features two small hills constructed out of World War II rubble, which have now been claimed by nature and both offer wonderful vistas across Berlin city centre for walkers and mountain-bikers.

📍

Volkspark Friedrichshain

🚋

Tram Platz der Vereinten
Nationen, Tram Paul-
Heyse-Strasse

Charlottenburg Palace Gardens

17th-century palace, surrounded by opulent gardens modelled on France's Versailles.

When Sophia Charlotte of Hanover married Frederich I of Prussia (after he lost his first wife to smallpox), Charlotte emerged as a formidable political force: her admirers included Peter the Great and Italian composer Arcangelo Corelli, who dedicated a series of violin sonatas to her. Charlottenburg Palace – originally christened Lietzenburg – was commissioned by the new Queen Consort of Prussia and is a Rococo masterwork that remains Berlin's largest palace to this day.

Whilst the palace today is a museum – much adored for its Rococo ballroom known as the Neuer Flügel and its silver vault, which features an historic collection of ornate tableware from the court – the grounds have become a refuge for strollers, sunbathers and hobby botanists. You can wander the geometrically sculpted gardens and expansive meadows beyond, intersected by the River Spree, meandering rills and small lakes. The grounds are also home to a charmed belvedere, a mausoleum (where Germany's first emperor Wilhelm I is interred) and a quaint cafe in the Orangerie.

The surrounding borough lends its name from the castle and is one of Berlin's more affluent quarters. Taking a stroll along the river in either direction to enjoy the peaceful surrounds and finely crafted architecture is highly recommended.

Spandauer Damm 20–4

U-Bahn Richard-Wagner-Platz, S-Bahn Westend, Bus Klausenerplatz

Mon–Sun
8am–9pm

Tempelhofer Feld

Ex-Cold War airport-turned-public space.

This city park is today a favourite meeting point for Berliners and tourists alike, but its dramatic Cold War history is enough reason to visit. Constructed in 1927 and expanded by the Nazi regime, Tempelhof Airport was, in the late 1920s, one of the world's most glamourous airports in the pioneering days of air travel. On 24 June 1948, however, the airstrip catapulted into infamy as the Soviet Union and East Berlin cut off water, land and air traffic to West Berlin, leaving it forsaken and with dwindling supplies. So began the largest airborne supply delivery in history: 200,000 flights over 15 months by pilots as far flung as Australia and South Africa, transporting in nearly 13,000 tons of essential supplies. Over 100 fatalities were recorded (both pilots and civilians) during the Berlin Airlift, and the airfield would become both a military and commercial hub during the frosty Cold War years, finally shutting in 1996.

In 2010 Tempelhof officially became a park, and is now a place for both relaxation and recreation in one of the world's most inimitable public spaces. While there are few formal activities as such, the site has become a recreational hub for locals and a pilgrimage for tourists keen to stroll, skateboard or rollerblade down its abandoned runways or simply relax in the sun with a bottle of beer and a good book amidst kiters and cavorters. On the weekend hundreds of Turkish families typically congregate here to grill up a storm and socialise.

Platz der Luftbrücke 5

Mon–Sun
6am–8.30pm

S + U-Bahn Tempelhof,
U-Bahn Platz der
Luftbrücke, U-Bahn
Leinestrasse

Wannsee

The city's most popular lake with forest,
palaces and a dark history.

Cornelia Froboess was just eight when, in 1951, she conquered the German
hit parade with *Pack die Badehose ein* (*Pack your Swimming Trunks*):
a frivolous song about frolicking in Wannsee. So if it's warm, do pack
your swimmers, as this vast lake has long been a summer playground for
Berliners: due to its historic open-air lido, or Strandbad, with pristine beach
sand imported from the Baltic coast, and a nude bathing section – known
colloquially as 'free body culture'. More than a shimmering sea of water,
however, Wannsee is the lungs of Berlin, surrounded by the verdurous forests
of Grunewald with its many walking and riding trails.

Highlights at Wannsee include the Pfaueninsel (Peacock Island),
with its dreamy castle that can be visited via ferry; the Russian church and
log villa (Nikolskoe), constructed for Tsar Nicholas I and his Prussian wife
Alexandra (now a restaurant serving up wild game and other Brandenburg
specialties); and the stately home of Max Liebermann: an Impressionist
German painter, whose graceful house is now a gallery and cafe much
loved for its country-style cakes. The Glienicke Bridge is best remembered
as the 'Bridge of Spies' – a famous photo spot. You can also explore the
House of the Wannsee Conference: the imposing mansion where the Nazi
leadership mapped out what they coined the 'Final Solution', now a museum
documenting the conference.

Königstrasse 3

S-Bahn Wannsee

Schlachtensee

Berlin's most sublime lake, surrounded by forest.

Berlin is one of Europe's greenest cities: surrounded by over 100 lakes and dense forests of beech, birch and chestnut. Every Berliner has a favourite lake: with the Müggelsee and inner city Weissensee perennial favourites. Yet few lakes prove as bewitching as the Schlachtensee in the city's south-west reaches: reputedly one of the deepest and cleanest lakes in the city (bursting with perch and bream) and certainly its most winsome. It's also a popular spot for stand-up paddle-boarding, and both boards and rowboats can be hired from the hut near the Schlachtensee train station.

The Fischerhütte (fisherman's hut, see p.137) at the northern end of the lake is ever-inviting, with its tiers of beer benches and freshly tapped Hefeweizen (a widely enjoyed German wheat beer) – a charmed place where you can watch swimmers and paddlers in the water (captured so serenely in Walter Leistikow's 1895 painting *Evening Mood at Schlachten*see). The hut also stocks bretzeln (pretzels) and sausages, and is famous for its Apfelstreuselkuchen (apple crumble cake). The adjoining Krumme Lanke lake is another Berlin icon, and the subject of Fredy Sieg's mischievous 1923 hit song *Das Lied von der Krummen Lanke* (*The Song of Krumme Lanke*). Both lakes can together be circumnavigated in around 1.5 hours, where you'll find yourself immersed in pristine nature and opulent wealth, with the lake being home to some of the city's finest stately manors.

📍

Am Schlachtensee 82

🚇

S-Bahn Schlachtensee,
U-Bahn Krumme Lanke

Treptower Park

*Historic countercultural meeting point
with a striking Soviet memorial.*

This is a park of pleasure and contemplation but also a place of palpable history. Reputedly more than 80,000 Soviet soldiers fell in the 1945 Battle of Berlin – a dogged month of hand-to-hand street combat between the Red Army and German Wehrmacht and Waffen-SS that ended with the suicides of Adolf Hitler (with Eva Braun) and Joseph Goebbels (with wife Magda and the murder of their six children) on 30 April and 1 May respectively, and total surrender on 8 May. The vast and stirring Soviet War Memorial in Treptower Park – constructed in 1949 – honours the fallen Soviet soldiers.

The second largest park in Berlin – after the Tiergarten (see p.201) – this riverside refuge of green has long been a local's meeting point and is today a veritable carnival of people on any day of the week: sunbathing, juggling, larking or taking a stroll beneath its plane tree-lined avenue. The Insel der Jugend (Island of Youth) in the River Spree is home to the Kulturhaus (culture house): a haven for progressive creative expression, including music and visual art. You can rent a boat from here to explore the placid waters, with a beer garden and food stands all nearby to satiate you after all that rowing.

Puschkinallee 15

Mon–Sun
10–1am

S-Bahn Treptower Park

LISTMANIA

Art and Berlin are truly synonymous. Few cities boast the creative calibre of the German capital, whose prodigious pedigree can be traced through literature and poetry, visual art, theatre and, of course, music across the spectrum – from classical and jazz, to punk and techno. But while the city has also given birth to countless home-grown masterpieces, it's also long been a beacon for outsiders: attracting everyone from David Bowie to author Christopher Isherwood, whose Berlin-inspired creations have gone on to be enjoyed by millions. And the city continues to inspire a new generation of cultural provocateurs. Here is your essential go-to list for a behind-the-scenes taste of Europe's cultural capital.

FIVE SONGS

David Bowie – *Where Are We Now*
While most people are quick to point to the anthemic *Heroes* as the defining song of Bowie's Berlin years, *Where Are We Now* (2013) finds the Thin White Duke on a deeply nostalgic stroll through the city of his memory: referencing landmarks, nightclubs, the Wall and even the KaDeWe (see p.59).

Marlene Dietrich – *Ich hab' noch einen Koffer in Berlin*
In 1937, at the height of Nazism, Germany's most famous film star made one of the toughest decisions of her life: to renounce her homeland and apply for US citizenship. Her ballad *I Still Have a Suitcase in Berlin* (1954) is a deeply beautiful tribute to the city of her birth.

Iggy Pop – *The Passenger*
In 1976 David Bowie moved to Berlin to try and conquer his cocaine addiction. His friend Iggy Pop soon joined him and enjoyed a prolific period of recording at Hansa Studios in Kreuzberg, by the Berlin Wall. *The Passenger* was written while riding the Berlin S-Bahn.

Pink Floyd – *A Great Day for Freedom*
Soon after the Berlin Wall tumbled, Pink Floyd's Roger Waters triumphantly performed the band's smash album *The Wall* at the very site. But just a few years later his bandmate David Gilmour began to question the new world order with this powerful reflection *A Great Day for Freedom* (1994).

Paul Kalkbrenner – *Train*
Berlin and techno are synonymous. What began as the fatalistic soundtrack to a lost generation quickly became the euphoric sound of a city now united in one epic party. DJ Paul Kalkbrenner emerged from this euphoric period. *Train* (2008) is a dedication to his city and its proud electro roots.

FIVE BOOKS

Hans Fallada – *Alone In Berlin (Every Man Dies Alone)*
It's 1940 and Berlin is under Nazi control. Following the death of their son on the front in France, an otherwise unassuming couple decide to subversively fight back against Hitler's machine. While fictionalised, this gripping 1947 novel is based on the true-life story of Otto and Elise Hampel.

Christopher Isherwood – *The Berlin Stories*
UK author Christopher Isherwood would come of age in the rousing Weimar era of Berlin (1918–33): a city of sin, booze and hedonism pre-Nazism. *The Berlin Stories* consists of two novellas: *Mr Norris Changes Trains* and *Goodbye to Berlin*, both which capture a thrilling city at its dramatic zenith and would later be adapted into *Cabaret*.

Alfred Döblin – *Berlin Alexanderplatz*
Murder, subterfuge, political upheaval ... what's not to like about this iconic tome? Published in 1929, *Berlin Alexanderplatz* remains the defining portrait of the confluence of two incongruous Berlins: between the imperial Prussia of the 19th century and the tectonic upheaval of the 20th century, rendered in a truly cinematic prose.

Thomas Brussig – *Heroes Like Us*
While Thomas Brussig found himself on the wrong side of history (being an East Berliner), he later found himself on the right side of literature with *Heroes Like Us* (1995), a hilarious and sometimes dark novel tracing the life of a wannabe Stasi informant in East Berlin's penultimate days.

Sven Regener – *Berlin Blues*
The Berlin Wall has collapsed, and the city has emerged as a sinner's delight. Indeed, the Berlin of the 1990s may have today entered the realm of folklore, but with Sven Regener's *Berlin Blues* (2001) – a witty tale of debauchery and wanton hedonism, readers can relive this unique period.

FIVE FILMS

Wings of Desire

Wim Wenders wasn't born in Berlin, but with *Wings of Desire* (1987) – a cinematic dreamscape, he portrayed its intimacies and unlit corners like few others. The film follows angels who plant themselves amidst the city's residents, revealing private tales of love and loss – and even catching a young Nick Cave in concert.

The Lives of Others

It is 1984 and Stasi agent Gerd Wiesler is set on a new mission: to spy on a playwright on the behest of the Minister of Culture. What unravels is one of the most gripping tales in German cinema history: its wide acclaim netting it an Oscar (2007), British Academy Award (2008) and a César (2008).

Die Sinfonie der Grossstadt

Released in 1927, *Berlin: Symphony of a Metropolis* remains a masterwork of German silent cinema. Part documentary, part avant-garde montage this film is set on a single day in Berlin across five acts, showing stunning motifs of a thriving city at work and at play, all set to a rousing score by Edmund Meisel.

Good Bye, Lenin!

It's October 1989 and Alex's mother Christiane has just suffered a major heart attack. While she is in a coma, the Berlin Wall collapses, and when she finally wakes the doctors warn Alex not to tell his patriotic East German mother the news for fear of another fatal attack. So begins a hilarious and heart-warming story of family and upheaval.

M

For many the genre of European Noir begins here, with this gripping thriller that Fritz Lang would cite as his masterwork. This 1931 production traces the spectre of a killer, the misuse of justice and the mob mentality. Filmed in Berlin during the rise of Nazism, it remains a cinematic classic.

FIVE ARTWORKS

Adolf von Menzel – *A Flute Concert of Friedrich the Great at Sanssouci*
Friedrich the Great's reign over Prussia (1740–86) was a defining period
in the kingdom's rise to global power. While marked by conquest, Friedrich
the Great was also a great patron of art and the Enlightenment and a keen
flautist and composer. This painting hangs in Alte Nationalgalerie on Museum
Island (see p.69).

Ernst Ludwig Kirchner – *Potsdamer Platz*
This vibrant work captures the full colour and movement of Potsdamer Platz
in 1914: then a global centre of fashion, wealth and entertainment. The area
would be totally erased by the bombs of World War II, and Kirchner too would
suffer a similarly harrowing fate: his works banned by the Nazis and tragically
he committed suicide in 1938. This work is shown in the Neue Nationalgalerie
near Potsdamer Platz (see p.91).

Max Liebermann – *View on Lake Wannsee*
Few artists represent the stark contradictions of Berlin quite like Max
Liebermann – a Jewish artist who would be declared an honorary citizen
of Berlin in 1927, just as the Nazis were on the ascent, and an artist whose
impressionist works reveal a tranquil paradise that would soon enough
become a dystopian warzone. This work can be found at the Liebermann Villa
at Wannsee (see p.213).

Käthe Kollwitz - *Woman with Dead Son*
Kollwitz' most enduring work – also known as *Pietá* – is a deeply moving
sculpture of a grieving mother holding her lifeless son, today housed in the
Neue Wache (see p.85), and inspired by the bereavement for her own son
Peter, killed in World War I. It remains a powerful symbol of the traumas of war.

Kani Alavi – *It Happened in November*
Iranian–German painter Kani Alavi had a front row seat to the fall of the Berlin
Wall from his apartment near Checkpoint Charlie. So in 1990 – when invited
to contribute a mural onto the now landmark East Side Gallery (see p.95) – he
painted what he saw that night: thousands of faces streaming through a crack
in the Wall and into a new world.

Listmania

THE ESSENTIALS

Whether you're visiting Berlin for the first time or you've discovered the city before, this chapter will guide you to travel like a local.

GETTING TO/FROM BERLIN

Plane

The city's much-delayed Berlin-Brandenburg Airport is set to open in late 2020, after originally being scheduled to open in 2011. Its delay is a sore point for a country notorious for its efficiency, but the airport will eventually handle an estimated 34 million passengers annually and be serviced by train, bus and taxi.

Until then, Berlin operates two niche airports. Tegel Airport, in the city's north-west, services most major international airlines and is connected to the city centre by bus and taxi (around €30). Schönefeld Airport, in the city's south-east, services mainly short-haul and discount airlines, and is connected to the city by train, bus and taxi (around €50).

Train

The Inter City Express (ICE) – Germany's high-speed train network – is a great way to travel for both efficiency and comfort.

Most ICE services arrive at Berlin Hauptbahnhof (central train station), a towering glass structure where you can easily connect onto U-Bahn (underground) or S-Bahn (rapid transit) inner-city and suburban lines.

The ICE is the best way to connect to other German cities for ease, including Munich (4–6 hours depending on connection), Frankfurt (4 hours) and Hamburg (2 hours). The ICE also serves many international destinations, including Prague (4.5 hours), Amsterdam (6–7 hours) and Warsaw (5–6 hours). There are also cheaper Inter City (IC) options, with longer travel times and older carriages.

All bookings can be made online at: www.bahn.com in multiple languages. Seat reservations are an additional cost (€4.50) and are recommended to ensure a seat on busy routes and on weekends. When travelling, you'll need to carry the ticket (or e-ticket) plus the credit card used to pay for it, which will be inspected by the conductor onboard.

THE ESSENTIALS

GETTING AROUND BERLIN

On Foot

Berlin is an eminently walkable city, with few hills and most streets pedestrianised. Mitte, the city's central borough, is perfect for ambling around on foot, whilst other boroughs are best reached on bike, train or tram and then further explored on foot. Pack comfortable shoes and a bottle of water and get to know the city's endless hidden corners. Tip: be wary not to stray onto the dedicated bike paths, as Berlin cyclists are numerous and often in a hurry.

Bike

Berlin is the definition of a biking city. Being flat, almost every resident owns a pair of wheels – and motorists are usually also cyclists, so are hyper vigilant to bicycle traffic. The city is well connected with dedicated cycling paths (watch out for stray pedestrians), which sometimes merge onto roads. Beware of crossing tram tracks – a perennial hazard to tourists unaccustomed to navigating these obstacles. Tip: cross the tracks on an angle to avoid your wheel getting wedged and bucking you off.

As a global tech-hub Berlin has a number of bike-sharing platforms (see: deezernextbike.com, mobike.com and li.me), but most hotels will also rent you a sturdy pair of wheels. Take heed of the innumerable bike carcasses strewn around the city and attach your bike with a lock to something sturdy and secure.

Car

In Germany, they drive on the right-hand side of the road. Germans are car-mad, and Berliners are no different – and are generally good, confident and respectful drivers. Tourists can legally drive for a consecutive total of six months on their own valid domestic driver's licence – however, beyond that you will need to apply for a German driver's licence (Führerschein, €40) at the local Rathaus (town hall) or Bürgeramt (municipal citizens' office). The website: howtogermany. com has some good tips on this and advice on driving in Germany as a foreigner.

Driving in Berlin is relatively easy by European standards, with clear signage and modern roads. Many older boroughs, however, still feature cobbled lanes, so take to these slowly to avoid an uncomfortable ride and also watch for occasional one-way and narrow roads. Berlin is encircled by a ring road, which services a number of Autobahns (toll-free freeways) to cities and towns beyond – many of which have no set speed limit (denoted by a sign showing a circle with a black stripe through it). Beware of wannabe race car drivers that can suddenly appear out of nowhere, often clocking 200 kilometres (124 miles) per hour plus. In other areas 130 kilometres (80 miles) per hour is the maximum speed limit. Within the city limits, you need to heed all parking signs: Berlin's Ordnungsamt (order police) are notoriously swift and unforgiving. Be vigilant of the many cyclists on the roads (especially when turning, as cars must give way to cyclists) and trams.

Trains

The U-Bahn (underground) or S-Bahn (rapid transit) inner-city and suburban train lines are incredibly efficient and have a comprehensive network, covering much of the city with multiple connections. U-Bahns are numbered 1–9 and cover 170 stations, many appreciated for their striking architectural designs. The S-Bahn generally runs above ground (except in the city centre) and stops less frequently – ultimately connecting with many areas in the city's outer limits. The Ring S-Bahn encircles the city and is often used as a tourist circuit. The S41 runs clockwise and the S42 counter-clockwise.

One ticket is valid across both U-Bahn and S-Bahn networks (plus trams and buses) and is denoted by three zones: A (inner city), B (outer city) and C (outskirts). Ensure you purchase the correct ticket according to the zones you'll

be traversing or you'll risk a fine by the plain-clothed inspectors. Tickets are one-way, last two hours, can be purchased at the station via vending machines (small change is most reliable) and must be stamped at the validating machines before entering the train. AB tickets cost €2.80, ABC tickets €3.40 and all-day tickets are €7.70 and cover all zones. See: www.bvg.de

Trams and Buses

A legacy of a divided Berlin the city is generally defined by buses in the West and trams in the East. Trams are a pleasant way to navigate the city – with the M10 route between the boroughs of Prenzlauer Berg and Friedrichshain particularly popular, as it passes through the heartland of the former East, including the Berlin Wall and the aweing Soviet-style architecture of Frankfurter Tor. The yellow buses are a fixture in the West and south of the city, and are frequent and reliable, thanks to dedicated bus lanes. Tickets can be purchased onboard both trams and buses – where they are immediately validated and last two hours (and also valid on U-Bahn and S-Bahn). Carry coins for both buses and trams. See: www.bvg.de

Taxi

While the train network is the cheapest way to get around town, taxis are ubiquitous, safe, honest and offer a chance to see the city above ground. The minimum taxi fare is €5 for a short trip. An app: Free-now is commonly used to order taxis in Berlin, although most hotels and restaurants will be happy to phone for one on your behalf. Taxis take most major credit cards but prefer cash. At the time of printing, ridesharing remains heavily restricted and uncommon in Berlin due to stringent taxi laws.

HOTELS

Like any major city Berlin has a range of accommodation options across all budgets, but here are some recommended hotels.

Michelberger
This Friedrichshain hotel brings together style and swagger to create one of the city's most memorable hotel experiences. Feel like a true Berliner as you waltz the lobby with sunglass-clad creatives and fabulous fashionistas, in search of your morning cocktail.
See: michelbergerhotel.com

Das Stue Hotel
This hotel takes its location in Berlin's diplomatic quarter to heart: a bastion of refinement and luxury, with stately rooms, regal appointments throughout and a staggering chandelier entrance with marble staircase – and views across the verdant Tiergarten (see p.201).
See: das-stue.com

25 Hours Hotel Bikini Berlin
Whereas once austerity dominated today 'new Berlin' is finally allowing itself to be (just a little) bold and brash. And few have embraced the zeitgeist quite like the Bikini complex in Charlottenburg, with boutiques, eateries and of course its flagship hotel overlooking Berlin Zoo.
See: 25hours-hotels.com

nHow
Berlin's partying pedigree is legendary, but no hotel embraces this fact quite like nHow in Friedrichshain. With a premium spot overlooking River Spree this ultra-contemporary hotel is fitted out with the rock'n'roll soul in mind: splashy, edgy and just a little bit kitsch. Live it up!
See: nhow-berlin.com

Lux 11
If location is everything, then Lux 11 has it all: situated right between Hackescher Markt (see p.183) and Alexanderplatz (see p.81) in Mitte, with access to all the key central Berlin sites by foot – and set in a resplendent 19th-century building once used by the KGB as a command centre.
See: lux-eleven.com

LIVE LIKE A LOCAL

Climate

Berlin has a classic continental climate, with erratic and regularly humid summers and long cold winters replete with occasional snow. In the cooler months you should pack for the full brunt of a North European winter – including stable footwear for likely snow, black ice and incessant rain. In the warmer months you should pack for all seasons: Berlin's summer is notoriously capricious, and languid balmy days can quickly give way to cool spells. In hot weather it is not uncommon to see locals stripping down to the bare essentials to soak up the summer rays in public parks.

Museum Pass

The Berlin Museum Pass is the best way to get the full sweep of this cultural capital. The three-day ticket is €29 and gets you into over 30 museums and galleries, including all the big hitters on Museum Island (see p.69). This ticket can be purchased online (smb.museum), which saves any queuing at ticket booths.

Eating and Drinking

Berliners can very much be divided into the old and new. Old Berliners will typically enjoy a small early breakfast of boiled egg, rye bread, ham and a pot of coffee before enjoying a large cooked lunch and then a soup or salad for dinner.

Young Berliners tend to kick off the day with a mid-morning brunch in one of the city's diverse cafes, with a barista coffee and organic juice blend. They then take their evening meal at one of the city's new breed of international eateries. Drinking here tends to kick off late – and it's not uncommon for friends to arrange 'early drinks' at 9pm before heading out to a bar, club or concert, only to re-emerge in the early hours of the morning. The 'all-nighter' is de rigueur in Berlin, and the morning streets wouldn't be the same without a few wobbly revellers.

While credit cards are becoming increasingly more widespread many smaller bars, cafes and eateries are cash-only, and it is always best to carry some in reserve.

LGBTIQ+

Berlin has long been a bastion of tolerance, and every year countless travellers flock to the city to enjoy its annual calendar of pride and LGBTIQ+ focussed events. The main Pride Day Parade – also known as Christopher Street Day – takes place in July and meanders through the city: drawing up to 750,000 revellers each year. The city administration publishes a calendar of LGBTIQ+ related events and tours, which can be accessed online at: visitberlin.de/en/lgbti-gay

KEY DATES

If you needed any proof of Berlin's ever-contradictory history then look no further than its public holidays, which celebrate everything from revolution to religion and reunification. Beyond these public holidays, some key dates include:

May 1 –
May Day

May Day in Berlin has a history of skirting the subversive edge, thanks to the city's large anarchist community and the legacy of socialism in the German Democratic Republic. Tens of thousands take to the streets annually – most often in peace and solidarity – to recognise the plight of workers and call for greater rights for working class Berliners in the face of increasing rent prices and gentrification. The streets around Kottbusser Tor in the district of Kreuzberg can sometimes prove a flashpoint for spontaneous rioting, as can Mauerpark (see p.171) in the district of Prenzlauer Berg – and both are monitored by a heavy police presence. But in general May Day is a chance for Berliners to celebrate their proud working-class roots.

May/June –
Karneval der Kulturen

This kaleidoscopic street party has been held annually in the district of Neukölln since 1996, celebrating Berlin's multicultural diversity and advocating for peace and tolerance. What started off as a modest celebration now attracts over one million revellers lining the procession route down Gneisenaustrasse. The parade ends at Hermannplatz, where the festivities spill over into Hasenheide park (see p.205), with bands, DJs, international food stands and much revelry. See: karneval.berlin

June 21 –
Fête de la Musique

This celebration of song may have begun in France, but Berliners have truly embraced it: trumpeting the beginning of summer. The annual Fête de la Musique sees musicians of all stripes storming the streets of Berlin to strike up a chord, and countless cafes, restaurants and bars jump onboard – setting up stages in every nook with free events, many of which are family-friendly. See: fetedelamusique.de

August –
Long Night of The Museums

What began in 1997 as a move to attract a new audience to Berlin's many world-class museums and galleries has evolved into one of the highlights of the city's annual calendar and has now been exported to other cities around the world, including Amsterdam, Buenos Aires and Paris. More than 30,000 people annually storm the turnstiles to enjoy the city's cultural treasures over a glass of wine. An average of 75 museums and galleries take part and doors stay open until 2am, with a series of parties hosted across the city. One ticket gets you into all venues with shuttle services from door to door. See: lange-nacht-der-museen.de

October 3 –
German Unification Day

This annual event marks the day East and West Germany formally unified on 3 October 1990, after the Wall was toppled in 1989. This family friendly street party takes place around the Platz der Republik, Strasse des 17 Juni and Brandenburg Gate (see p.87), with entertainment, food and drink stands and memorials. See: tag-der-deutschen-einheit.de

October –
Festival of Lights

Many say Berlin only truly wakes up after dark, and that's certainly true of the annual Festival of Lights. Running over 10 nights at over 100 locations across the city – amongst them the Brandenburg Tower, Berlin Cathedral and TV Tower – international light artists descend on the city and set about bringing its most iconic buildings to life. The Festival of Lights is particular popular with families. See: festival-of-lights.de

December –
Christmas

In Berlin Christmas is not a day … it's a full-blown season. In early December you'll notice workers setting up wooden cabins across the city, which soon after transform into stalls selling Glühwein (mulled wine), roasted chestnuts from the city's native trees and grilled bratwurst. Christmas fever hits its peak in the weeks leading up to Christmas, as the city squares are transformed into enchanting Weihnachtsmärkte (Christmas markets – see p.181), selling handcrafts, artisan wares and Christmas treats, such as sugared almonds and steaming cherry beer. The city administration publishes a full calendar of Christmas markets and festivities. See: visitberlin.de/en/christmas-markets-berlin

DANKE

Thank you to Hardie Grant for its enduring support throughout this project: to Melissa Kayser for proposing the book and having faith, Megan Cuthbert for her indefatigable counsel and Alice Barker for her erudition and ever-faultless eye: it has been the greatest of pleasures. And I doff my hat to Lila Theodoros, whose handsome designs have brought these pages to life – and equally to all the photographers whose images inspirit this book.

To both sides of my clan: the antipodean (Erica and Allan) and the Teutonic (Hildegard and Gerhard), I'm infinitely grateful for your resilience to my boundless flights of fancy and – as ever – your sage advice and support.

To that ever-enigmatic city: thank you for inviting me in on a fraction of your mysteries. All these years later I continue to wander your cobbled lanes in awe. To call you home is a true privilege indeed, and one I endeavour to never take for granted.

And ultimately to my dearest, Sarah, Maxime and Philomene. Thank you for gifting me the codes to your natal city and enduring my restlessness, roaming and rambling throughout this project (and beyond). This book is for you.
Wir haben immer einen Koffer in Berlin.

Published in 2020 by Hardie Grant Travel,
a division of Hardie Grant Publishing

Hardie Grant Travel (Melbourne)
Building 1, 658 Church Street
Richmond, Victoria 3121

Hardie Grant Travel (Sydney)
Level 7, 45 Jones Street
Ultimo, NSW 2007

www.hardiegrant.com.au/travel

A catalogue record for this
Book is available from the
National Library of Australia

Wanderlust in Berlin
ISBN 9781741176476

10 9 8 7 6 5 4 3 2 1

Publisher
Melissa Kayser
Senior editor
Megan Cuthbert
Project editor
Alice Barker
Editorial assistance
Rosanna Dutson and Jessica Smith
Proofreader
Helena Holmgren
Design
Oh Babushka
Prepress by Splitting Image Colour Studio

Printed and bound in China by LEO Paper Group